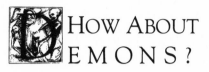

How About
Demons?

OLKLORE TODAY
Linda Dégh, General Editor

How About Demons?

Possession and Exorcism in the Modern World

Felicitas D. Goodman

INDIANA UNIVERSITY PRESS
Bloomington and Indianapolis

Manufactured in the United States of America

Library of Congress Cataloging-in-Publication Data

Goodman, Felicitas D.
  How about demons?

  (Folklore today)
  Bibliography: p.
  Includes index.
  1. Demoniac possession.   2. Exorcism.   I. Title.
II. Series.
BF1555.G66   1988   291.2'16   87-45403
ISBN 0-253-32856-X
ISBN 0-253-20467-4 (pbk.)

  2 3 4 5   92 91 90

To my grandchildren

Charles Andrew
Eleanor Amy
Sarah Daniels
Andrew Murphy
Jason Ananda
Seth Joshu

ONTENTS

Foreword

> Every time we acquire knowledge we enlarge
> the world, the world of man, by something
> that is not yet incorporated in the object of
> the knowledge we hold, and in this sense a
> comprehensive knowledge of man must ap-
> pear impossible.
>
> —Michael Polanyi, *The Study of Man*

Folklore Today, the title of this new series, is more meaningful than it would seem at first glance. It not only implies the reportage of current trends in the discipline of folklore, information on the latest findings and thoughts of scholars, but, more important, it addresses the presentation of new, or old but earlier unrecognized, folkloric phenomena and the research methods and theories that resulted from their discovery and investigation.

Folklore, as a constituent segment of culture, is a dynamic force in any permanent or temporary population group of modern complex societies. It appears as an endless continuum, relating the past with the present and aiming at the future. Thus, it emerges as a historical process in which tradition and innovation play equally important roles, although they do not always appear in equal measure. The folklore corpus of a given social group is an intricate complex of old, new, and restored personal and communal elements in diverse stages of integration and disintegration. Tradition accommodates, shapes, adjusts, and at the same time promotes new ideas following the dictum of actual needs. The interdependence of the two results in both the solidification of universal formulas and the creation of innumerable local-temporal variables. Hence, no new creation can be understood without familiarity with the previous stages, or indeed the total process. But if folklore is a process to be viewed diachronically, it is also a product of existing social conditions to be examined empirically in the context of the cultural, economic, technological, and ideological present responsible for its actual formulations. The dialectic relation of these two characteristics of folklore calls for an interdisciplinary extension of approaches, essentially historical, sociological, and anthropological. The books in this series will demonstrate the benefits of placing the science of folklore between the social sciences and the humanities.

European and American schools of folklore became increasingly more aware of the need of this extension, particularly prompted by the radical and speedy transformation of folk culture after the end of the Second World War. A new generation of scholars took issue with the premises that called folklore into existence in the nineteenth century and that had dominated its trends up to the first four decades of the twentieth. Research goals of this discipline were subjected to national interests and maintained an essentially ethnocentric-romantic bias, preventing scholars from developing an objective scientific inquiry. The folk was understood as the lowest layer of society, which in its underprivileged condition unconsciously preserved the genius of nations expressed by the great poets of a distant golden age. Consequently, the lore of the folk gained national prominence, and its research (serving the practical goal of indoctrination in order to restore and strengthen national cultural unity on the basis of historic values) was celebrated as an ideological discipline. Folklore as heritage: primitive or naive aesthetics was regarded as a model for artists to create an original national art; folklore as ideological weapon was to set the patterns of a distinctive national identity whereby independence and political power would be achieved. Restoration, revitalization, and broad public application of carefully selected archaic folklore under the guidance of professional folklorists grew into a mass movement nationally as well as internationally. As a result of the interaction of the folk, the folklorist, the applier, and the consuming public, we experience the boundless dissemination of folkloric phenomena. The academic, the applied, and the recreational mass use and manipulation of accessible, indigenous, as well as relocated folklore materials, taken from various sources, ensure the flow of folklore from the folk through several hands back to the folk for screening, regeneration, and perpetuation.

The recognition that folk and folklore exceeds earlier narrow confines and that folkloric and nonfolkloric phases cannot be separated from each other within the processes of transmission, spread, and transformation in society prompted modern folklorists to divert their interest from the past to the present. Following a critical evaluation of the history of the discipline, the so-called new folkloristics focuses on the ethnographic present and the folklore emerging from the observable complex interplay of folk, mass, and everyday culture. Switch from the past to the present, noted Bernd Jürgen Warneken, considerably strengthened the methodological sophistication of folkloristics and catapulted it from the last row of disciplinary development into the very front.[1]

The idea of breaking away from historic reconstruction of an eclipsed folk culture from its rudiments and turning to the current life of people in the country and in the city was launched already in the early thirties.[2] A more systematic step toward establishing *Gegenwartsvolkskunde* (present-day folklore), however, was made only following World War II. As a consequence of the war events and conditions of the immediate aftermath, political and socioeconomic changes led to the transformation of labor relations, lifestyle, ideology, and forms of recreation. The relaxation of the rigid social hierarchy also resulted in migration and resettlement, and opened the door to upward mobility with increased choices of careers. The traditional (peasant) folk experienced the greatest change through mechanization and commercialization of farmwork. While peasantries lost their "folk" hallmark, they traded in their traditional values, bringing about a so-called peasantization of general society as it was noted by ethnographers. This means that with the industrialization of the rural folk, old folklore forms did not vanish, but in adequately applied form they became the shared property of social groups within nations. New present-oriented research is committed to tackle such specific social constellations and emergent cultural forms on the basis of empirical observation.[3]

It seems evident that folkloristics had to give up its original claims to fulfill its mission in the modern world, which, in addition to the transformation of the agricultural masses, has experienced never-before-anticipated cultural consequences of population explosion, and the homogenizing effect of mass information and consumer service through advanced electronic technology. Modern sophisticated tools are needed to investigate folk society and culture, framing creative processes of the contemporary folk. The creative fantasy of the folklorist, so much in action during the romantic era, does not work anymore to help the interpretation of folklore. We have to ask the folk about the realities of the world.

This suggestion was already made eighty years ago. Lajos Kálmány (1852–1919), village parson and pioneer collector of oral literature, was on good terms with his parishioners. He was a jolly peasant priest who helped with the harvesting and gave a hand when the pigs had to be neutered. His Sunday school was fun for the children. Instead of listening to religious exhortations, they wrote their jingles and stories into a copybook. In an era of search for the mythopoetic age, Kálmány devoted his time to individual storytellers and singers. Record-

ing repertoires, he did not discriminate the genuinely oral text from
materials of literary origin. He studied the process of folklorization of
foreign elements. In doing so, he came to the understanding that the
folk poet's perspective departs from the present reality of his world
and that the messages contained in poetic utterances are existentially
relevant. In his scattered notes and unfinished essays, Kálmány carefully documented this observation:

> Those who are experienced by doing long-term fieldwork must have
> noticed that the folk is the poet of the present. The folk does not look
> back, does not attempt to recall historic events of past centuries for
> poetic inspiration like professional authors do. The folk is profoundly
> concerned with its own fate and uses only the materials that address its
> problems. This is the reason why the folk is selective and would
> maintain materials from its ancestral heritage only if they are adaptable
> and filled with meaning in its own world.[4]

Regrettably, the recognition that folk societies in subsequent historic
epochs created their own folkloric expressions on the basis of their
social reality comes too late to remedy the scantiness of our knowledge
about the processes of tradition. However, case studies of new, con-
spicuous forms of folklore as they evolve before our eyes in response
to current social events not only may tell us more than ever of the
nature of folklore transmission, but also may open a new era for
folkloristics, proving its usefulness as a most sensitive parameter of
the dimensions of human creativity.

In this series, then, we will introduce new folkloric phenomena, as
well as new approaches and theories that were developed in the
course of their study. It is in the nature of folklore that its student is,
either by birthright or by vocation, an active participant in the creative
process with all ambiguities of the involved eyewitness. Subjectivity
and commitment of the observer, however, do not mean weakness but
rather strength, the ability to distinguish between one's own heritage
and one's target of study.

We are fortunate to open the series with the study of a universal
belief concept that is basic to individual expression of awe and to
systems of religious institutions. From shamanistic rites to medieval
mystic cults, authoritative practices of modern western Catholicism,
fundamental Protestant sectarianism, and configurations of Third
World Christian churches incorporating native religions down to non-
institutional, nonreligious beliefs, all contain the element of spirit
possession. Felicitas Goodman's book *How about Demons?* is about
possession and exorcism: belief and ritual in the modern world. But is
this belief and practice relevant to our reality, and if so, why? Average
enlightened people would normally view exorcism as a Catholic

church ceremony of long ago, irrelevant to concerns of today. But the fact is that despite (or because of?) advanced technological sophistication, affluence, and the improvement of the quality of life, irrational belief is proportionately growing in the modern Western world—fear from demonic possession, in particular, as it became clear after fictionalized versions for the shock-hungry, bored, blasé reading and moviegoing audience became overnight bestsellers. The symptomatic proliferation of possession belief with or without Christian overtones, however, is not confined to members of religious sects. The press is the most dependable indicator that possession became a household ill in the eye of the public and exorcism a credible method of healing. No sensationalization but succint and dry factual reportage is characteristic of such news items in the daily papers:

The criminal court in Danbury, Connecticut, held hearings on a stabbing murder case attributed to devil possession (*New York Times,* 1981); a woman sued TWA for physical injuries suffered by her when her twin sister died in a crash (UPI, 1983); Jesuit Karl Patzelt successfully exorcised a young couple and their two-year-old son in San Francisco (*Der Spiegel,* 1974); a high-school teacher routinely exorcises her pupils in Fallbrook, California (*Louisville Courier Journal,* 1974); a possessed three-year-old girl keeps her family in anguish in Gillingham, England (*Winnipeg Free Press,* 1985); twelve-year-old Annette Hasler in a small Swiss village was beaten to death when a priest and her parents exorcised her (*Time,* 1973); a twenty-month-old boy died when his mother put him into a hot oven in New York during an exorcism rite (UPI); seventy-four-year-old Madame Esnaut in Normandy, regarded by some as a saint, by others as a witch, was convicted because she injured a man tormented by evil spirits during exorcism (*General Anzeiger,* 1977, Bonn).

It seems the underlying belief in evil spirit possession is *nolens-volens,* confirmed by the authoritative practice of the Catholic church and the Church of England. Chief Exorcist Bishop Neil Smith of the Church of England reported more than one thousand cases of possession annually, while the Catholic Rituale Romanum is performed routinely by appointed regional exorcists—Father Jean Bosco was recently named as exorcist for the diocese of the Swiss Kanton Wallis (*Aargauer Tagblatt,* 29 March 1986). After all, in Christian culture norms of good and evil are established and taken for granted. One does not have to be a religious zealot, not even an occasional churchgoer, to accept the underlying mythology that if God exists, his antagonist, Satan, must also exist, and that the struggle between the two concerns our well-being.

The case study of Dr. Goodman is an eye opener to the fact that the nature, life, and function of modern folklore phenomena cannot be understood by extricating them from their social base. The basic idea appears in variable forms, in folkloric and nonfolkloric situations. Canonic belief, philosophy, psychology, and scientific inquiry are as much a part of it as personal experience, fear, and cultural tradition. The ethnographic observer is limited in many ways to go beyond description and assumptions. He can open a window to inspect the universe of human expressions, but the horizon is restricted by the size of the window, and the glass is often blurred. Raising questions on the basis of so far acquired knowledge, even if the answers are not fully satisfactory, leads to clarification of issues and more knowledge.

LINDA DÉGH

NOTES

Foreword

1. Utz Jeggle, Gottfried Korff, Martin Scharfe, and Bernd Jürgen Warneken, *Volkskultur in der Moderne* (Hamburg: Rowohlt, 1986), p. 15.
2. Max Rumpf, "Vergangenheits- und Gegenwartsvolkskunde," *Kölner Vierteljahresschrift für Soziologie*, vol. 9, pp. 407–429.
3. Hermann Strobach, "Literatur zur volkskundlichen Gegenwartsforschung" (a bibliographical overview), *Deutsches Jahrbuch für Volkskunde* 11 (1965), vol. 2, pp. 343–86.
4. *Történeti énekek és katonadalok,* collected by Lajos Kálmány (Budapest: Közoktatási Kiadóvállalat Budapest, 1952), p. 92.

Preface

To many viewers of the film *The Exorcist,* which ran for months in American movie theaters a few years ago, the story was merely a horror tale. The audience could sit back and enjoy it because such things could not possibly happen. However, in the summer of 1976, just a few years after the release of the film, a case of exorcism made headlines around the world. According to the reports in the mass media, a Catholic German university student by the name of Anneliese Michel contended that she was possessed by demons. When treatment by the family physician and various psychiatrists brought her no relief, the bishop of her diocese gave permission to two priests to carry out the ritual of exorcism. Despite their efforts, however, she was not cured, and several months after the attempt at exorcizing her was abandoned, she died. A German court of law charged her parents and the two priests with negligent homicide for not forcing her to accept more medical treatment and sentenced all three of them to suspended jail sentences.[1]

The German popular press had a field day, sensationalizing the supposed "horrors" of the exorcistic ritual and the attendant belief system as hopelessly outdated, medieval superstitions. "Only in the backwoods of Bavaria," was the battle cry. However, the ritual of exorcism is by no means confined to provincial Catholic congregations. It is well known around the world, not only in Christian but also in many non-Christian, non-Western religious communities as a treatment for extreme psychological and physical discomfort involving in severe cases life-threatening depression, loss of appetite, and frenzied rage. In a religious ambient it is thought to result from some malevolent spiritual entity penetrating into the individual. The experience in question is termed *possession,* and in fact, exorcism cannot be properly understood without first describing the condition it is designed to cure, namely, possession.

Both possession and exorcism are important features of modern life literally around the world, and the subject has been treated extensively in the literature. The present volume does not presume to give a comprehensive presentation, which would require a much more voluminous work. Its goal is instead to provide an overview of a topic that has for many years excited the imaginations of people from all walks of life. As such, it is an undertaking of modest scope, and by no means all sources could be discussed or, even less, quoted. Although I tried to select those that are considered important and authoritative, my personal preferences could not entirely be suppressed. So to those who may find their favorite author slighted, I extend my apologies. I also beg the indulgence of those who may become impatient with me for spending so much time in the first chapter on the physiological processes, the bodily changes, that persons undergo during a religious experience. However, much of that is new, and attractive just for that reason. Also, I admit to being partial to this topic, because some of it concerns my own research. But quite aside from this fact, I am honestly convinced that it is important to the understanding of possession and exorcism, as for that matter of any religious experience, to realize that humans react as total beings, body and soul, and not as some disembodied spirit floating in a vacuum. Some theologians of my acquaintance are deeply committed to the latter view, most certainly because they never had a religious experience to speak of. But the evidence speaks against them. For what we see instead is that changes in the body and perceived experience are inseparable aspects in possession, as in any other bona fide religious experience. The cross-cultural agreement in physiological changes marks us as members of a single species. The significant differences in perceived experience illustrate how strong we are shaped by our respective cultures, our belief systems. Contemplating possession and exorcism in a holistic manner by paying attention to both these aspects will underline its reality and help us to restore dignity to a topic that has too long languished in the bonds of "superstition" in the public view. To this goal the present volume is fervently dedicated.

I owe a debt of gratitude to many colleagues and friends: to Erika Bourguignon, once a teacher and now a cherished friend, who started me on the path toward these inquiries; to my consultants in fieldwork, especially in the Apostolic congregations in Yucatán; to my coworkers and helpers in the laboratory; to the psychologist Colin Pitblado and to the psychiatrists Ralph B. Allison, David Caul, and Frank W. Putnam, Jr., who answered my questions and guided me to the relevant literature; and to Willard Johnson, who read and offered helpful comments on the initial draft.

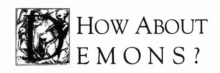 HOW ABOUT
EMONS?

1 POSSESSION'S MANY FACES

In order to understand possession, we need first of all to come to terms with the concept of the *soul*. The behavioral sciences, such as psychology or anthropology, consider human beings to be bio-psychological systems. According to this view, all experience results from the interaction of the various parts within this integrated unit. Obviously, there is no room for the soul in a theory of this sort. As Virchow, a famous German surgeon of the nineteenth century, used to say, "I never found a soul with my scalpel." We may ask, of course, whether the scalpel is the most useful tool for finding the soul. Ancient sages as well as religious specialists active in societies today the world over, including our own, certainly never used it for that purpose. They simply took the existence of the soul for granted, building their entire belief system on the conviction that indeed humans do have at least one or possibly even several souls.

The two opinions are clearly at loggerheads with each other, and although as Westerners, we are inclined to opt against the soul theory, we should at least be fair and ask the following question: If you disagree with the idea that humans are integrated systems, a heap of cells having unimaginably complex interconnections as well as psychological dimensions, but nothing else, then what are you going to propose as a countertheory? The answer we will get from those cleaving to the "soul hypothesis" is that in their view, humans consist of a shell, something like a box, namely, the body, and an ephemeral substance or essence residing within, usually termed the soul. All the various religious faiths and systems we are going to become acquainted with in these pages take the soul theory for granted, as a given, as their unshakable foundation.

To clarify some of the ramifications of the soul theory, let us couch it in some seemingly simplistic imagery: for those accepting the soul hypothesis, a human being could be likened to a car with a driver in it. The car is the body, and the driver is the soul. This simile makes it easier for us than any theoretical discussion could to understand what people mean when they talk about the experience of possession. Just as the driver owns the car, so the soul owns the body. The owner of the car drives the vehicle, and it is the soul that activates the body. Now, suppose the driver has a friend who has no car. What might happen? The driver, if he is so inclined, could invite this friend temporarily to take over the wheel and to drive the car. In terms of the soul theory, something of this sort happens in possession. In a religious ritual, this supplicant asks a being of the other, the alternate, reality, who possesses no physical body of its own, to descend into his/her body for the duration of the ritual and to use it as it sees fit.

The question is, what happens to the owner soul when such an alien being takes over its body? To understand that, let us return to the car and its original owner. While his friend drives the car, the owner or host may stay in the back seat, for instance, just watching. He may praise his friend's driving skill. Or perhaps his friend wants to have the car to himself for a while and so asks the owner to get out. Any one of these things may happen with respect to the interaction between the soul that has proprietary rights to the body and the incoming spirit. The choice is a matter of cultural configuration.

Some ethnographic examples will illustrate the point.[1] The Yąnomamö Indians live on the border between Venezuela and Brazil.[2] When they are intoxcated with *ebene*, their hallucinogenic snuff, they sing to their *hekura* spirits, miniature, glowing beings that live in the jungle, to come and live in their chests. The following is a brief section of an account given by their ethnographer, Napoleon Chagnon, who joined in one of their rituals:

> My arms seemed light and began moving almost of their own accord, rhythmically up and down at my sides, and I called to Ferefereriwä and Periboriwä, hot and meat hungry *hekura* and asked them to come into my chest and dwell within me. I felt great power and confidence, and sang louder and louder, and pranced and danced in ever more complex patterns. I took up . . . arrows, and manipulated them as I had seen . . . shamans manipulate them, striking out magic blows, searching the horizon for *hekura*, singing and singing and singing. Others joined me and still others hid the machetes and bows, for I announced that Rahakanariwä dwelled within my chest and directed my actions,

and all know that he caused men to be violent. We pranced together and communed with the spirits. . . . (1977:158)

One gains the impression in this description that the soul of the shaman and the tiny jungle spirits share the space in the supplicant's chest as equal partners.

But when the Holy Spirit possesses a Pentecostal worshiper, the body "turns into a tabernacle,"[3] as one member of such a congregation told me, and the "owner soul" dwindles into nothingness. I was struck by this impression once more when during fieldwork in a village in Yucatán in January 1985, a member of the Apostolic congregation there reminisced about his first experience of speaking in tongues:

> You know how it is: You see it happening to others and you wonder, will it ever happen to me too? And then it does happen. I was praying for this manifestation of the Holy Spirit. All of a sudden I started trembling, and without wanting to, my lips began to move and the sounds came tumbling out, and there was light all about and I knew nothing more.

And there may even be a conflict between the owner of the body and the spirit that would like to take it over for the time being. Siberian shamans tell of knock-down, drag-out fights between their souls and an invading spirit. As the Hungarian folklorist Vilmos Diószegi described it,[4]

> The spirit that is about to take up its abode in the body of the shaman starts battling with the shaman's own soul; it tries to suppress it and force it into submission. Frequently, the [invading] spirit does not succeed until after a prolonged and vicious struggle. That is why the start of the experience, of the total ecstasy, is preceded by lengthy agony, by nervous trembling, dizziness, and vomiting. When the spirit is finally victorious, the shaman's soul has been fettered and silenced; it can say nothing at all. Instead, it is the spirit that penetrated that does the speaking, that acts and moves by using the shaman's body. (1958:331)

From these descriptions, the reader might gain the mistaken impression that a takeover of the owner's body by some spirit entity can happen any time or any place. Or, speaking in terms of the car and its owner, somebody casually ambling down the street could simply jump in and steal the vehicle. But matters are not that simple. Possession can come about only if certain very specific preconditions are met. The most important of these is a separate entranceway for the spirit into the car.

To understand this precondition, let us think of the mythical car we have been talking about as having a rather singular feature. Only its owner can enter by the ordinary front door. Guests need a special one of their own, a spirit door, if you will. When considering its various features, we come to realize that this entranceway is truly miraculous. Let us examine it a bit more in detail.

The Spirit's Fingerprints.

By this we mean first of all that not just any spirit can be involved in a particular possession. It has to be the *right* spirit. That is, the respective spirit is "culture-specific." Normally, *hekura* spirits can enter only during a Yąnomamö ritual. The Holy Spirit comes to worshipers during a ritual in a Pentecostal church. A *hekura* or a Siberian shaman's spirit would not appear in such a temple.

The Spirit's Key.

Second, a door will not open without a key. The key to the special spirit entrance is the ritual preparation and a specific cue. As to preparation, Yąnomamös put on some special feather decoration. In a Pentecostal church, there are particular hymns addressed to the Holy Spirit, asking for its "fire," for instance. Then people go to the altar and kneel down. In Siberia, all the relatives gather, a festive meal is prepared, and gifts to the spirit are placed on an altar. The special cues for the spirit's arrival are hardest to detect for an outside observer. It is not difficult to note that for the Yąnomamö it is the inspiritation of the hallucinogenic snuff. But in a Pentecostal prayer, it may be anything—a particular phrase, such as, "Oh, my God," or even just a particular impression or memory called up by the person in prayer. Siberian shamans, on the other hand, often assume a particular posture.

The Spirit's Door.

The spirit cannot enter until this very complex key is actually in place. But what now about the door itself? This door is marked "trance." Put differently, the only way a spirit, an alien entity, can take possession of a human's body is if that body first undergoes certain specific changes, an alteration of consciousness termed *religious trance* or *ecstasy*. When these changes happen, humans begin to act in a nonordinary way. There might be dizziness, trembling, convulsions, even a dead faint. That is quite disconcerting to Western-trained anthropologists, who may be tempted to interpret what they see in psychiatric terms. Isn't such behavior hysteria, or epilepsy?

Anthropologists know, of course, that within the religious specialists' own culture, these people are considered "normal." But for
centuries, and clear into the present, religious practitioners that were
observed when going into trance have been classed in Western literature, be it of psychiatry, psychology, or comparative religion, as
mentally ill. It is understandable that even in the minds of anthropologists, who from their participation in the life of non-Western
societies should have known better, the suspicion lingered: Was it not
possible nevertheless that the shamans, the mediums, the priests in
non-Western societies behaving so strangely were actually psychotic?

In order to answer this question, Erika Bourguignon, professor of
anthropology at Ohio State University, undertook a five-year large-
scale statistical study beginning in 1963 with the support of the National Institute of Mental Health.[5] Using the Human Relations Area
File, a vast repository of ethnographic data, she and her graduate
assistants counted the occurrence of the religious altered state of
consciousness or trance in small, non-Western societies of interest to
anthropology. They included its expression not only in possession but
also in other cultural behavior, such as spirit journeys, visions, or
divination. Given the large number of societies that anthropologists
have made a record of, it would be an unlikely coincidence indeed if
each one of these societies, despite their small size, at all times possessed the right kind of psychotic person of the right sex and the right
age to carry out its religious rituals, if indeed that was the case. In
other words, if one had to wait for such a coincidence to occur, there
could be only a small number of societies using the religious trance.
The majority of societies would have to forego the institutional use of
this altered state. However, that was not what the statistical study
showed. It demonstrated instead that nearly all the societies examined
included some form of religious trance in their rituals. In one sample
alone of 488 societies, for instance, 437, or ninety percent, had one or
more institutionalized, culturally patterned forms of the religious
altered state of consciousness. As Bourguignon points out,

> [This] represents a striking finding and suggests that we are, indeed,
> dealing with a matter of major importance, not merely a bit of anthro-
> pological esoterica. It is clear that we are dealing with a psycho-
> biological capacity available to all societies. (1973:11)

The significance of this statistical study was that it freed researchers
interested in religious trance behavior from the burden of having to
start over and over again trying to prove that ecstasy did not represent
any pathology. They could begin looking at it as the expression of a
ubiquitous, perfectly normal genetic endowment instead. The follow-

ing discussion will provide an overview of some of the research based on this insight, viewing the religious trance or ecstasy as a general human psychobiological capacity.

I became interested in ecstasy initially because I was doing research on a behavior observed extensively both in Christian and in non-Christian religious observances, namely, *glossolalia,* a vocalization called in the congregations of the Pentecostal movement "speaking in tongues." Frequently, such vocalization consists of syllables that are "vacuous," not carrying any meaning, such as, "lalalalala," "ʔulalala dalalala," or "tsetsetsetse." After carrying out a careful linguistic analysis of tape recordings of such vocalization by speakers of various English dialects, I found that the utterances shared a number of features that were not encountered in English, or in any other natural language, for that matter. Each syllable began with a consonant, if we included the consonant called a "glottal stop" indicated in the second example quoted above by a "ʔ." They were rhythmical to an extent not heard even in scanned poetry. Because of this rhythm, individual utterances had more in common with music than with natural language; this impression was heightened by the fact that as the result of an accent pattern, each utterance was subdivided into bars of equal length. And most important, all utterances shared a common intonation pattern, which rose to a peak at the end of the first third of the unit and then sloped gradually toward the end. Figure 1 clearly shows the characteristic shape of such a glossolalia curve, traced by a level recorder in a phonetics laboratory.

Features such as accent, rhythm, and intonation are called suprasegmental elements in linguistics, because they float, one might say, above the syllables, the segments. In subsequent fieldwork with Spanish speakers in Apostolic (Pentecostal) congregations in Mexico City and with Maya-speaking Indian congregations in Yucatán, Mexico, I found that their glossolalia had the same suprasegmental elements as that of the English speakers. Tape recordings later supplied by helpful colleagues[6] of glossolalia from a non-Christian sect, a so-called New Religion (see chap. 3), in Japan, from spirit mediums in Ghana and Africa, and even from a woman healer among the headhunters in Borneo who is calling her helping spirit, demonstrated that these suprasegmental features were unfailingly present. When we remember that all these people under ordinary circumstances speak very different languages that are not related in any way, it is logical to conclude that what we are hearing here has little to do with language. Put differently, the uniformity of the suprasegmental traits of glossolalia cross-culturally and irrespective of the native tongue of the speaker suggests that we are dealing with a neurophysiological change

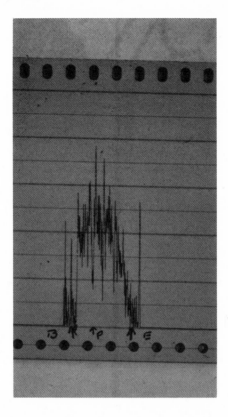

Figure 1. "Speaking in tongues" of a member of the Streams of Power
congregation of St. Vincent Island. B = beginning; P = peak;
E = end. (Bruel and Kjaer level recorder, Model 2304, paper
speed 3 mm/sec)

that is instituted in all religious ritual when humans speak in this
nonordinary way. The syllables themselves are probably created in the
speech area we have in the left side of our brain. But other than that,
those suprasegmental elements we have been talking about are so
alien to ordinary language that they must be produced by something
else that is happening in the speaker. This impression was strengthened further as I listened to the so-called interpretation of the glos-
solalic utterance that is mentioned in the Bible as one of the "gifts of
the Spirit." It is not practiced in the Mexican Apostolic churches, but I
heard it often during fieldwork in various Evangelical temples in this
country. It had a pleasing rhythmical quality to it, and this rhythm
occasionally got in the way of grammar, so that a syllable would get
lost at the end of a phrase, or a word would break in half. The level

recorder revealed a perfectly regular wave pattern for the intonation of this interpretive speech, with each wave once more exhibiting a rather flat peak at the end of the first third of the unit.

I suspected early on during my research that the "something" affecting the mode of speech was the change wrought in the body by the religious trance, and this supposition was amply confirmed by field observation; no matter in what kind of ritual it happened or where, people speaking in tongues always showed the same characteristic behavior, sometimes minimally, sometimes very clearly. Quite generally, while people vocalized in ecstasy, some did not appear much different from the ordinary. Usually, however, their faces seemed drawn and flushed. There might be strong perspiration and a flow of tears or of saliva. There was evidence of considerable muscle tension, and they might tremble or twitch. Now, if people behaved the same way cross-culturally while speaking in this nonordinary way, that is, in glossolalia, it was fair to assume that they all entered only this one altered state and no other while vocalizing in religious context.

If we now compare what happens physically when there is glossolalia with the way people appear when they are possessed, we find that there is really not much difference. So we can propose with some confidence that this particular trance is the only altered state of consciousness that occurs in religious context generally. That is an important point, because actually, ecstasy is only one of a large number of different altered states of consciousness that humans can assume. Others are sleep, for instance, or the hypnotic state, or the meditative ones. Before we had enough information about ecstasy, there was a great deal of confusion about what exactly we were dealing with. Each one of these altered states of consciousness mentioned has at one time or other been a candidate for explaining religious experience. It was thought, for instance, that a spirit journey took place during sleep, that it was a dream. Or that the religious trance was the same as the hypnotic one. Because of their special history, as we shall see, this was a view propagated especially by the Spiritualists. And in many Christian circles, "contemplating" God, that is, meditation, is thought to be ecstatic, because of the "oceanic" feeling some people have experienced. However, there is clear evidence in research that ecstasy differs from all of these other states, and that in all probability, there is only one ecstatic state.

The question we now want to ask is, what happens in the body, especially in the nervous system, during ecstasy? Modern research has provided important new insights in this area. Some interesting conclusions are suggested first of all by observation. For instance, the glossolalia utterance's suprasegmental elements act like a window on brain activity. The strictly rhythmic quality of glossolalia, its intonation and segmentation, tell us something about what goes on where these patterns are created, someplace in our nervous system. The utterance is a summation of those patterns, the way a sentence is a summation of a number of different grammatical rules that need to be applied before it is finally spoken. In some hidden reaches of our body, an activity is triggered that is pulsing, the way our heart does, and this pulsing rises to a peak and then drops, only to start over again, until the initial impulse is spent, as when a bell is struck, rings for a while, and then falls silent again. In addition, a command must also be issued someplace within the speaker that says: contract, release, contract, release, because that is what the structure of a glossolalia syllable demonstrates. As I mentioned above, it starts with a consonant, which involves a muscle contraction, and ends with a vowel, which is produced by relaxation, letting the air escape freely.

We do not yet know exactly where all these commands originate. The research of biologist Charles M. Fair[7] suggests that the sympathetic and parasympathetic nervous systems may both be involved. They stand in an "answering effect" relationship to one another, so that if parts of one are activated, parts of the other will respond. That, I think, might account for the alternating tensing and relaxing effect we observe in glossolalia. Barbara Lex, a medical anthropologist, attributes the fact that people feel so well and relaxed after an ecstatic experience to this action of the nervous system.[8] The alternate tensing and relaxing of this system, she thinks, kneads it and releases accumulated tension. At any rate, the excitation produced during the trance can be very intense. I once filmed a young man in an Apostolic congregation in Mexico City who while speaking in tongues jumped up and down from a kneeling position so rapidly that the film gave the impression of having been taken at time-lapse.

This intense excitation can also have psychological consequences. Observers never cease to be amazed at the creativity that people show during and after a trance of this nature. I have heard hardworking, taciturn Maya Indian peasants, who in ordinary life had difficulty uttering two coherent sentences in public, bringing forth poetry of surpassing beauty in ecstasy. Japanese religious leaders write truly enormous volumes of religious thought, again often in poetic form, while possessed by their deity, as we shall see. And the pronouncements of demons, thought to speak from the mouths of the possessed, have been quoted by emperors and popes.

In addition to observation, laboratory tests can also add importantly to our understanding of the neurobiology of ecstasy. My coworkers and I undertook such testing in 1983 at the University Neurological Clinic in Munich, Germany, in connection with a doctoral dissertation in medicine.[9] There were four experimental subjects, two trained by me in the techniques of ecstasy, and two who had never experienced this altered state of consciousness. My technique involves driving by the rapid beating of a gourd rattle, while the subject assumes ritual postures known from the ethnographic literature.[10] Recording of the test results before, during, and after the ecstatic experiences, each lasting fifteen minutes, was done electronically in order to safeguard against human error.

To briefly summarize the test results, we found that in the blood serum, adrenalin, noradrenalin, and cortisol at first increased slightly and then dropped below initial values. Simultaneously, there was an increase in beta-endorphin, which persisted beyond the end of the session. This is the body's own pain killer, and is responsible for the joy, the euphoria, experienced after the ecstasy. Blood pressure dropped, but pulse rate increased at a furious rate, "like an athlete's during a hundred-meter dash," as one of the physicians interpreting the results observed. The EEG indicated not the presence of alpha waves, so often associated with nonordinary states of consciousness, but the predominance of theta waves. "Remarkable," the EEG specialist[11] termed it, "normal adults don't show these theta patterns when awake." Phenomenologically, the experience of ecstasy is classed as an awake state, so the appearance of theta waves is especially striking.

As maintained above, humans apparently utilize the same kind of trance for ritual purposes the world over, which suggests that it is part of our genetic endowment. It is therefore not surprising that it gets rediscovered even without access to any tradition. That is what happened in Spiritualism and with the Pentecostal movement, as we shall see in chapters 2 and 4. It also explains why some people stray into it seemingly by accident. A famous example is the Swedish visionary Emanuel Swedenborg, whom we are going to discuss in the next chapter. Accidental onsets of ecstasy are on occasion preceded by dramatic experiences, dreams, visions, convulsions reminiscent of epilepsy, or periods of amnesia. In anthropology, this is known as "shamanistic illness." In small, non-Western societies, a person whom it befalls is seen as one chosen by the powers of the alternate reality for a life as a religious leader.[12] Andrew Jackson Davis, one of the important early thinkers of the American Spiritualist movement (see chap. 2), spontaneously passed through this series of experiences.

While the ability to go into trance is genetically transmitted, it needs to be triggered in some way in order to be available for ritual purposes. Straying into it is rare. Usually, ecstasy is consciously induced and represents a learned behavior. Religious communities where it is practiced either rely on repeated demonstration during ritual as a teaching device, or have rituals expressly designed to lead the beginner into it. In most non-Western societies, being able to switch into ecstasy easily during certain rituals is a prerequisite of adulthood. A person who cannot do it is considered defective, suffering from some mental aberration. One purpose of the widely reported initiation rituals for the young is permanently to condition the nervous system to take this step in response to a ritual cue.

In order for the switch from the ordinary perceptual state to the ecstatic one to take place, people first of all have to prepare physically. They fast, take a ritual bath, or purify themselves in a sweat lodge. At the ritual itself, the expectation that something extraordinary is about to happen is a powerful conditioning factor. But mainly, people need to concentrate. Trained practitioners do that as a matter of course; other have to learn it. I heard many an urgent sermon on this point in the Apostolic temples where I did fieldwork. Concentration is aided by the festive air and by whatever sensory cues may be customary in the particular religious community—music, drumming, singing, the fragrance of incense or of crushed aromatic herbs, flickering candles, or bright lights. However, concentration alone will not do it. Only very knowledgeable practitioners can change their perceptual state without any external help. Such help is termed an induction strategy, most of the time involving stimulation, an excitation directed at the nervous system, a certain "driving" provided by rhythmic activity.

Entering into ecstasy under ritual guidance and with the help of driving or another induction strategy is perceived by many practitioners as a more or less clearly marked transition, like stepping across a barrier, a point where a marked change takes place. The observer can also note it because of the sudden change in physical appearance of the religious practitioner, as mentioned above. Yet not all control is lost. Mothers never drop their infants, for instance, while moving quite impressively during ecstasy. A minimal channel is also kept open for perceiving outside stimuli. Although people in ecstasy tend to draw closer together, they do not bump into each other; neither do they stumble over obstacles.

The open channel for outside stimuli, no matter how narrow it may be, also facilitates the return to ordinary consciousness. All rituals contain signals for that to happen. Sometimes it is simply the cessation of ritual activity, a stop to the singing, for instance. Or there is a more emphatic sign. In the Mexican Apostolic churches, the minister would strike a strident little bell when he wanted to go on to the next part of a worship service. The return to ordinary consciousness is not always instantaneous; the ecstasy tends to linger, but eventually everyone manages to switch back to ordinary awareness. Soon after, many participants are rewarded by a sudden, intense rush of joy, of euphoria, reminiscent of what they mystics of another age must have meant when they described their experiences as "sweet."

Above, we used the simile of the door for characterizing the trance. A spirit can enter into the "car," into its human vehicle, only if the special entryway has been readied. We can then say that as long as the vehicle is guided by its owner and chugs along on an ordinary highway, we are witness to a scene from ordinary reality. However, when all of a sudden that mysterious door appears and a spirit enters, the events are no longer taking place in ordinary reality; they have been transported to the alternate one. Or in other words, when the functioning of the body is altered in this special way, namely, in ecstasy, that particular person gains the ability to come in contact with beings and events of another reality, with the sacred dimension. It is for this reason that, not surprisingly, many non-Western societies consider ecstasy the highest, the truly human, state, and the ordinary state of consciousness just that: ordinary.

The Experience of Possession

Up to now, the comparison between the car and its driver, on the one hand, and the body with its soul, on the other, has served us well as we try to comprehend possession. But we shall have to abandon this useful simile as we come to the next thing that happens. For while in ordinary reality the car will not change its appearance or functioning, no matter who drives it, that cannot be said of the body possessed by a spirit. Rather, astounding things begin to occur. The Yąnomamö shaman in whose chest the *hekura* has taken up residence is no longer the same person he was before. His facial expression is radically different; he moves as he would never do in ordinary life as he prepares to eat the souls of the children of enemy villages; even his voice is unrecognizable. The Pentecostal worshipers who receive the Holy Spirit into their bodies speak in wondrously rhythmical syllables that are unintelligible to the congregation. And from the Siberian shaman's mouth, a spirit may announce its presence, giving its name and telling those assembled about the shape of things to come. Rarely will a practitioner of this sort remember afterwards what took place.

It will be instructive at this point to discuss a specific possession complex in some detail. To do that, let us look at voodoo, or more correctly *vodun*, the folk religion of Haiti. *Vodun* has its roots in African ceremonialism and theology, having been brought to the island by African slaves. Through the centuries it was also significantly influenced by Catholicism. We will not describe all the features of a *vodun* ceremony, which is very complex indeed. Instead we will concentrate only on those features important for understanding the phenomenon of possession. The presentation is based on the field-work of Melville J. Herskovits, an American anthropologist and dean of African studies in this country.[13]

Of the many different *vodun* ceremonies, the one seen most often in the rural areas of Haiti, is a *vodun* dance. It is held regularly every Saturday night, and possession by *loas,* or deities, is its principal feature. Typically, people gather at the home of a particular family. Coffee is brewed, a group of drummers begins to play, the *houngan* or ritual specialist arrives, and soon, people begin to be possessed. To the careful observer, a number of stages become obvious at this point, namely, the entrance into the trance, the manifestation of the *loa,* its identification, and the dissolving of the possession. Let us look at each one of these a bit more closely.

The entrance into the behavior is characterized by the participants, the future "horses" of the deity as they are popularly known, becoming dazed, stiff, possibly going into convulsions. "As his possession comes on, the devotee falls to the ground, rolling before the drums, or staggers blindly about the dancing-space" (Herskovits 1971:184). Next, it becomes necessary for those present to find out which *loa* is present, because "to be possessed by a *loa* means that an individual's spirit is literally dispossessed" (1971:147). In other words, the possessed person does not know whose horse he has become, and has no way of speaking for himself. He has become, as it were, inoperative. To discover which *loa* is present is, however, of vital interest ritually, for each deity demands his or her own drum beat and songs. Herskovits describes the scene:

> As he [the possessed] appeared, the drummers stopped the Ogun rhythm they had been sounding, and in an intense silence all waited for the god to announce himself. Half on his knees before the drums, the one possessed began to sing in a cracked voice:

> > Damballa Wedo
> > Papa, I am a serpent-o
> > There is no tree
> > I cannot climb.

> With this initial statement, the Damballa rhythm rolled from the drums, as all echoed the song in chorused response. (1971:187–88)

The spiritual entity has taken over, and in doing so, "a radical change takes place in accordance with the nature of the possessing deity" (1971:147–48). In the example quoted above, the possessing *loa* was Damballa, a snake deity, who writhes on the ground and might climb a tree. Other *loas* behave differently:

One woman, possessed by Ogun, greeted all present first by shaking
hands with wrists crossed in the customary manner, and then kissing
each person on both cheeks. Another, possessed by Ossange, took the
neckerchief from about his neck and wiped the faces of all those
present, paying particular attention to the drummers. The son of the
family head was . . . possessed by Gede . . . and his greeting to the
assembled company was especially dramatic. His possession took the
form of a hysterical, rapid, continuous jumping, with the body held
rigid. As he bobbed up and down, holding his candle under his chin so
that the light distorted his features and emphasized the vacant stare in
his eyes, he monotonously repeated the sharp sounds of his god: *"ke-ke-
ke-ke-ke-ke-ke!"* or *"Hoi! Hoi! Hoi!"* (p. 196)

In the course of a single ceremony, which often lasts all night, a
person may even be possessed by a succession of deities, each exhibiting totally distinct behavior. Possession dissolves at the conclusion of
the dance. It should be clear from what was quoted above that
Herskovits was deeply impressed by the change that the "host" person
underwent as he/she became possessed. "Radical" he calls it, obviously
searching for the most fitting adjective.

It goes without saying that onlookers witnessing such extraordinary
behavior are at a loss about how to interpret what they saw. Some
anthropologists like to speak of role playing during possession ceremonies. In fact, that is the explanation most often advanced in the
literature. In Erika Bourguignon's words,[14] "Possession offers alternative roles, which satisfy certain idividual needs, and it does so by
providing the alibi that the behavior is that of the spirits and not of the
human beings themselves" (1976:40). In other words, in this view the
participants in a *vodun* ceremony just described are fine actors and
change their demeanor in keeping with personal needs and social
expectations. Less polite observers, especially of the Freudian school,
speak of auto-suggestion and self-hypnosis, aided by a willing audience, or of downright faking.

On the face of it, the interpretation of possession as role playing
seems very attractive, principally because it violates no cherished no-
tions about how things are, or are supposed to be: there is really
nothing out of the ordinary going on, just some ignorant or super-
stitiou people playing games. But there are those anthropologists,
such as Herskovits, who, after witnessing scenes like the ones described above, obviously are not so sure that this is all there is to it.
Faking seems out of the question in view of the sacred nature of the
rituals involved. More important, these religious practitioners undergo such radical changes during possession that it is difficult to
credit mere acting ability, no matter how outstanding, and even if
aided by "auto-suggestion and self-hypnosis," however that might

work. One comes away with the distinct impression that something more incisive is going on, not role playing but transformation.

How such profound alteration could come about, no one could even guess. Our ethnographic consultants, the people in the field who are willing and able to talk to us about their own culture, their religious experiences, the *hungans,* medicine men, shamans, mediums, Pentecostal speakers in tongues, all point to the presence of spiritual beings as sufficient explanation. But while accepting the validity of their experience for them, being Westerners, we still yearn for something more tangible, more "real." In other words, we wish there were something scientifically testable that we could point to. The problem is that our science was developed to test propositions of ordinary reality. We cannot test for the presence of spirits. Our only hope is once more that as in the case of ecstasy, there might be some parallel physical process that would not be as illusive as spiritual beings, and that would provide us with an explanatory framework. Until recently, the possibility of discovering anything of that nature seemed pretty remote. It is hard to imagine a shaman being wired up in the laboratory. In the last few years, however, psychiatrists have produced some research results concerning the so-called multiple personality disorder, which just might have some relevance to our problem.

The research in question concerns a diagnostic category termed *multiple* or *split personality* syndrome, a subcategory of the dissociative disorders. Patients of this type exhibit not one personality, like the rest of us, but several, which they experience as inhabiting them. This will immediately call up possession as we discussed it above, a similarity that did not escape a number of researchers.[15] The condition is relatively rare, and frequently it does not come to the attention of the psychiatrist until there is trouble, such as a conflict with the law. A famous case that is still occasionally in the news is that of Billy Milligan, who in 1976 was brought to trial in Ohio for rape, robbery, and kidnapping and was acquitted by reason of insanity. The insanity plea was based on the claim that he was a "multiple," that is, that he had a number of distinct personalities, only one of which was responsible for the criminal acts he was charged with. He needed treatment, not punishment. The American reading public became aware of this disorder in the 1950s through a monograph, *The Three Faces of Eve,* by two psychiatrists, Corbett H. Thigpen and Hervey M. Cleckley.[16] The book contains a wealth of detailed and well-reported observations, which further strengthen the impression that the phenomenon of multiple personality is similar in many aspects to that of possession. The report describes a young woman who showed evidence of having three personalities: the sedate, prim, and timid Eve White, her core

personality; the frivolous, irresponsible, and yet fascinating and
bright Eve Black; and the mature, thoughtful Jane.

Eve White came to Dr. Thigpen seeking help because she was
suffering from severe, what she called blinding, headaches. Here is a
brief description of the impression she initially made on her psychiatrist, before he was aware of the true nature of her complaint:

> She did not at first appear to be unusual or a particularly interesting
> patient. This neat, colorless young woman was, she said quietly, twenty-
> five years of age. In a level, slightly monotonous voice she described
> the severe headaches from which she had suffered now for several
> months. . . . Demure and poised, she sat with her feet close together,
> speaking clearly but in soft, low tones. (Thigpen and Cleckley 1957:1)

Now let us witness the scene when for the first time, the physician
comes face to face with Eve Black, her "coming out" or manifestation.
The similarity to what happens when possession sets in is quite striking here. Eve White had come to his office once more, because for
several months she had been hearing a voice "when no one was there."
She struggled to describe the experience adequately, and a minute or
two of silence ensued. Then,

> The brooding look in her eyes became almost a stare. Eve seemed
> momentarily dazed. Suddenly her posture began to change. Her body
> slowly stiffened until she sat rigidly erect. An alien, inexplicable ex-
> pression then came over her face. This was suddenly erased into utter
> blankness. The lines of her countenance seemed to shift in a barely
> visible, slow, rippling transformation. For a moment there was the
> impression of something arcane. Closing her eyes, she winced as she
> put her hands on her temples, pressed hard, and twisted them as if to
> combat sudden pain. A slight shudder passed over her entire body.
>
> Then the hands slightly dropped. She relaxed easily into an attitude
> of comfort the physician had never before seen in this patient. A pair
> of blue eyes popped open. There was a quick reckless smile. In a bright
> unfamiliar voice that sparkled, the woman said, "Hi, there, Doc!"
> (1957:20)

Eve White was gone, and another, totally different personality
calling herself Eve Black had taken her place, a change accompanied
by the peculiar headache, that is, by a perceivable physical event. Eve
White, the mousy, restrained, modest host personality, suffered a
blackout; she became as "inoperative" as the Haitian *vodun* practitioner described above. She had not the faintest notion what mischief
this saucy, seductive, debonair double of hers might be up to, or even
that she existed.

This new personality gave her own name, just as the *loa* did in *vodun,* and became identifiable to the therapist not only by her actions but also by the thoroughgoing transformation she worked in Eve White. Everything changed when she appeared on the scene, facial expression, muscle tone, voice, posture, motion patterns, and attitudes, just as in Haitian possession, where the emergence of the *loa* radically changed its "horse," the person possessed.

Where the phenomenon of multiple personality differs from possession, however, and this is an important point, is in ritual control. As explained above, nothing happens haphazardly in a ritual. *Vodun,* as we have seen, is not simply a chaotic possession event. People assemble at a certain spot; external preparations have to be completed; the appropriate point in time for the possession to start is marked by certain unmistakable signals in the ceremony. It is conceivable, although of course in no way proven, that the reason why so many multiples, including Eve White, report a severe headache when switching to another personality is that they do not have this kind of ritual help. One of my informants, for instance, had a comparable experience. In the temple, she often spoke in tongues, slipping into the behavior easily and effortlessly, stimulated by the induction going on about her, that is, under ritual conditions. She was able to duplicate that also in private prayer. However, as she told me, lying in her hammock one night, she was praying to God in tongues for a better understanding of the Bible, and the switch to a more intense experience came about spontaneously, and certainly was not smooth:

> All of a sudden, instead of going to sleep after praying, my head began hurting terribly, as if it was going to split in half, and I saw a great light. I could not stop praying [in tongues] until two the following morning. (Goodman 1972:61)

In addition, the *vodun* gods are permitted to come only to the members of the family giving the dance. As Herkovits remarks, "Possession occurs according to well-defined rules and under specific circumstances" (1971:143). What is perhaps even more important in view of the problems multiples have in trying to rid themselves of their unwelcome alternates is the fact that on ritual cue, the possession will unfailingly dissolve. Eve White, on the other hand, had no power over either Eve Black's emergence or her exit. In time, Eve White's therapist did gain a measure of ritual control over Eve Black, being able to call her up at will by pronouncing her name. But he could not prevent her from coming out also at inappropriate times, when her wild doings contributed to the conflict between Eve White and her husband and on numerous occasions caused her to lose her job. He most certainly could not cause the unwelcome alternate to disappear, which would have meant a cure. In this respect, the multiple personality disorder acts very much like demonic possession.

As happened also in the case of possession, the syndrome of multiple personality was interpreted by many health practitioners as being nothing but role playing, possibly used by clever fakers to escape from uncomfortable or threatening social situations. Nearly thirty years were to pass after Eve White appeared in the psychiatrist's office before this widely held opinion could be refuted with some confidence, when the neurophysiological correlates of the startling transformations undergone by multiples were finally identified in the laboratory.

The research leading to the discovery that there were observable changes in the brains of patients claiming to possess several personalities was carried out by Frank W. Putnam, Jr., a psychiatrist with the National Institute of Mental Health, and reported in 1982.[17] The results were confirmed by Colin Pitblado, a psychologist who formerly worked at the Institute of Living in Hartford, Connecticut, and is now with Post College in Waterbury, Connecticut. The researchers utilized a well-known property of the nervous system, namely, that it will instantly react to a certain stimulus, such as a flash of light, with a weak but identifiable change at particular spots on the cortex, the outer layer of the brain. This reaction is called an *evoked potential,* and it can easily be produced repeatedly and registered by electroencephalography (EEG). After the resulting pattern is amplified and averaged with the help of a computer, a curve of such evoked potentials can be drawn. The intriguing property of such patterns is the fact that they are very stable, in the sense that they are, one might say, permanently attached to a particular person—or, it would probably be more correct to say, to a particular personality, because Putnam found, for instance, that the patterns of various obsessive-compulsive patients tended to be similar. It was this stability that formed the cornerstone of Putnam's and Pitblado's research. If multiples, they asked themselves, were not gifted actors or fakers, but rather truly represented an assemblage of distinct personalities, would that not perhaps show up in differences of the pattern formed by evoked potentials?

As Dr. Putnam described the experimental setting,[18] the patient, accompanied by Dr. Putnam and the patient's therapist, occupied a well-insulated chamber, which as a fixation point had a flashing strobe unit. The patient had electrodes glued to his skull, one of them in the area over the visual cortex. The therapist then produced one or the other of several alternate personalities of the patient by calling out their names and watching for the changes in muscle tension and for other behavioral clues characteristic for that particular personality, thereby verifying its presence. The strobe light was turned on, the evoked potentials were recorded electroencephalographically, and the resulting pattern was analyzed.

The results indicated that the alternate personalities of a multiple had their own characteristic patterns that varied significantly from each other. Not only that, but comparing the pattern of the obsessive-compulsive alternate personalities of multiples with that of patients with the same personality structure but who were not multiples, the researchers found them to be very similar indeed. But when, instead of patients, Dr. Putnam tested control subjects who had carefully created and rehearsed in detail alternate personalities, their role playing in no way affected their evoked-potential patterns, which remained the same throughout the trials. Neither were the several patterns recorded from one particular patient affected by the passage of time, as Dr. Pitblado found when he tested the four alternate personalities of the same multiple over an interval of fifteen months. The alternate personalities remained in evidence, and so did the related brain organization as represented by the pattern of the evoked potential. It is especially instructive when instead of curves of the evolution of the EEG tracings over time, we see such differing brain organization represented in the form of maps. These maps, which look a little like various liquids poured over the brain near the top of the head which then spread and form different patterns, were produced from the EEGs of three different personalities of the same patient by recording evoked electrical potentials from sixteen electrodes placed on the skull. The spaces between the points were filled in by mathematical calculation.

Do multiples and those possessed experience the same types of changes neurophysiologically? To date it has not been feasible to carry out tests on persons in spirit possession similar to those reported above about multiples. However, as pointed out, there are impressive similarities between various aspects of the behavior of subjects experiencing multiple personalities and those possessed by spirits. Here are some additional agreements.

There is some indication that not only the possessed but also multiples experience trance. For example, some of the alternate personalities of a multiple, Eve Black in the case of *The Three Faces of Eve*, for example, as well as the spirit personality coming to the fore in a possessed *vodun* practitioner, are highly excited, hyperaroused. Eve Black "sparkles"; she sings and dances; her muscle tension is heightened. The *vodun* practitioner, his muscles extremely taut, equally dances, or keeps jumping up and down, as Herskovits observed.

Multiples and those possessed easily induce their condition in others, who may be nothing but bystanders. Thigpen tells of an

incident where Eve White was a patient in a hospital. Unexpectedly
Eve Black "came out" one day, as she said, just to look around in the
psychiatric ward. She came across a male patient who had recovered
from a bout with alcoholism and got him to dance with her. Although
the encounter was brief because a nurse took Eve back to her room,
the male patient spoke repeatedly and at length about the experience.
What disturbed him most was not so much that the gentle and demure
Mrs. White was all of a sudden an entirely different person, but that
he had had such a curious reaction to dancing with her: "Though he
was not exactly dizzy, the floor and walls seemed far away and he
found himself unsure of his balance" (1957:79). In other words, his
own perceptual state had been altered: the walls had not moved far
away; he had experienced or perceived that they had done so.

This kind of induction phenomenon by association, as it were, is
widely reported in the ethnographic literature. Herskovits mentions
an incident where a man had no intention at all of becoming possessed. In fact, there were strong cultural strictures working against
his participating in the experience. In social class, he considered
himself above the villagers, and his (Catholic) priest had earnestly
warned against contact with any "false gods." Yet just being present at
a *vodun* dance produced a highly agitated possession in him. For those
experienced in trance behavior, it is even more difficult to resist the
effect:

> In trying to resist their god . . . men have been seen holding so
> tightly to the rafters of the shelter under which the dance was being
> held that the muscles of their forearms formed great cords, while
> beads of perspiration rolled down their foreheads. (1971:149)

Along with hyperarousal, facial expression alters radically, and
there is a change in muscle tension. Dr. Putnam (personal communication) considers increased muscle tension to be one of the most
telling external signals for the "arrival" or coming out of an alternate
personality in a multiple. That is, multiples and those possessed have
this in common also, that both their bodies (muscles, facial expression)
and their behavior (in the form of hyperarousal) change under special
circumstances, the multiples when a particular alternate personality is
"out," and the religious practitioners when they are possessed. And if
we remember that Eve Black perceives the world not the way Eve
White does, but quite differently, and that the *vodun* practitioner in
possession sees the world as a Yoruba god would, also changed, that is,
we are justified in maintaining that both the patient and the *vodun*
dancer are in an altered perceptual state, in trance.

There is one revealing difference between the two phenomena, though, alluded to several times before—while for the *vodun* dancer possession begins at a ritually marked moment and ends at the conclusion of the ritual, there is no such control for the multiple. It is for this reason that with admirable logic, in Haitan culture *vodun* possession is not considered a disorder; it is expected and approved behavior. Quoting Herskovits once more, "In terms of Haitian religion, possession is not abnormal, but normal" (1971:148). It is equally correct from this point of view, namely, as regards the governability of the condition, that multiples in our society are classed as patients.

We might now speculate in the following manner. Let us assume that on the neurophysiological level, we are dealing with two manifestations of the same human capacity. In the case of the *vodun* dancer, in traditional possession, the map is created under the effect of the ritual and then dissolves at the proper time. That is, possession constitutes a manipulation of brain processes that can be learned. In the case of the multiples, the phenomenon is not intentionally initiated. Simultaneously, the resulting brain map is etched deeper, and it is for this reason that it eludes the control of the therapist. Is there any support for such a view in *vodun,* for instance?

There is indeed. A person might be possessed "accidentally" by an unruly, unauthorized spirit, a *loa bossal.* Such an "unruly" being is very difficult to control, and there is an impressive ritual, termed a "baptism," that needs to be performed in order to "tame" it. In other words, here we may be dealing with a brain map that comes about not during the proper ceremony but for undetected reasons, and that is more resistant to ritual control than the ordinary ones instituted as a learned behavior. Some milder forms of demonic possession could be ranged alongside this *loa bossal* experience. So we might think of the entire phenomenon as representing a continuum. On the one end is the learned and ritually controllable possession; at the other end is demonic possession together with the multiple personality disorder. We will pursue this line of reasoning further in chapters 6 and 7.

The last topic we want to consider now is that of healing, for all the various religions we are going to come to know in the following chapters claim to be able to perform miracle cures, that is, healing that seems to fall outside of what conventional Western biomedicine can reasonably be expected to achieve. Some of the claims one reads about are no doubt exaggerated. But many cases of faith healing have indeed been authenticated, and the service of the restoration of health in the many possession cults around the world is so successful— witness, for instance, in the case of Spiritualist healing in Mexico[19]— that we have to ask, Why do such cures work?

The answer given by medical anthropologists tends to be that the so-called folk healers get to treat mainly minor neurotic and psychophysiological disorders, as well as physical disabilities with emotional correlates. The reason the cures are successful is that the healer is aware of what problems are present in his/her society, and is able to gear the treatment to those circumstances. Much is made of the so-called placebo effect, or that attention is simply shifted away from the symptoms to other areas. Such theorizing presupposes adult, conscious patients, however. It would not account for successful healing in cases where the cultural factor is of minor or no importance. I should like to relate two stories from my fieldwork here to illustrate the point.[20]

The first incident concerns an infant. In the spring of 1970, the six-month-old son of one of the members of the Apostolic congregation where I was doing fieldwork in Yucatán (Mexico) contracted a severe respiratory infection. The worried mother took the child to the government clinic in the village, but the treatment was without effect. The attending physician told the mother that he could do nothing more for the little boy, that he was dying. So she brought the child to the temple and placed him, rigid, cold, and barely breathing, into the arms of the preacher. He prayed for him for about an hour, holding him in his arms. Increasingly, color returned to the infant's cheeks, his breathing became stronger, and he started to move. The respiratory ailment disappeared and did not recur.

The second story deals with a woman on her deathbed. The Apostolic minister, well known to me, of a village congregation near La Venta, Tabasco (Mexico), was called to pray over a dying woman. She was barely conscious, her extremities were cold, and her perspiration felt sticky. Some members of the congregation had been praying for her, but there was no reaction from the patient. The physician had left, saying that there was nothing more he could do. In the words of the minister,

> We prayed for a few hours, then some of us decided to go and rest and return at sunrise. There were only a few Brothers left at the dying woman's bedside when I came back at daybreak. Their faith had become weak. "We prayed and prayed," they said, "but God has not heard us." Again we started praying, and continued for half an hour. Nothing. Finally I said, "Lord, I am not worthy to place my hand on her, but perhaps you will choose to act through me." So I put my fingers very lightly on her forehead, saying, "May the Holy Spirit work on you." Not five minutes later she began to speak. She is still living, taking care of her six children.

What the two reports have in common is the apparently instantaneous effect of the minister's touch, in one case holding the infant, in the other case touching the dying woman's forehead. As we shall see, healing in the various possession religions involves either touching, such as laying on of hands or massaging, or "irradiation," where the healers hold their hands up with palms turned toward the patient, or else pass them over the client's body, close to it but without touching. The observations suggest that the healers induce the beneficial, healing trance in their patients.[21] That would indicate that they "radiate" something, we have no name for what it is, that calls up a resonance in the body of the client. A few preliminary laboratory experiments indicate that such is actually the case. In research with Oskar Estebány, a well-known Canadian faith healer, it was found, for instance, that if he held surgically wounded mice, they healed faster than if control mice with the identical lesions were kept at the same temperature as that of his hands, or if randomly selected medical students held them.[22] A biochemist determined that the faith healer in question could also affect an enzyme called trypsin. If he held a test tube containing it, it showed an increase in activity as if it had been exposed to a strong (8,000–13,000 gauss) magnetic field.[23]

The research on the role of brain maps in multiples may also contribute to our understanding about healing in possession cults. Consider the following observation reported by Thigpen. In a comparison between Eve White and Eve Black, he writes,

> Eve White: No allergy to nylon has been reported.
> Eve Black: Reports that her skin often reacts to nylon with urticaria. Usually does not wear stockings when she is "out" for long periods. (1957:132)

In other words, Eve White has no urticaria, a skin rash, that is, an allergic reaction, when she wears nylon hose, and Eve Black does. As we know, in terms of research that was done a generation after Dr. Thigpen observed Eve White, what distinguished Eve White from Eve Black was not that they had different bodies—they "inhabited" the same one—but that they were associated with different brain maps. The logical conclusion is that the allergic reaction was part of only Eve Black's map. Neither are allergies the only difference between alternate personalities reported by psychiatrists of their multiple patients. There are many other diseases, as well, headache, for instance, and functional bowel disease, that only one of the alternates may suffer from. Anecdotes are also reported that one alternate personality may react to a certain drug quite differently than another. David Caul, an Athens, Ohio, psychiatrist, tells (personal communication) of a patient whom he gave a heavy dose of barbiturates. There was no reaction whatever, until an alternate personality came out. Instantly, the patient "dropped like a stone." So we might speculate that those truly

miraculous remissions of severe illnesses that are sometimes reported
may come about under treatment by faith healers if they not only
induce the religious trance in their patients but also succeed in producing a change, a rearrangement or possibly even a substitution of
the brain map. This point brings to mind that in some parts of
Austria, folk healers are called *Wender,* those that "alter," or "turn
things inside-out." It is an appropriate term for a curer of this kind.

Exorcism, which will occupy us repeatedly throughout this book, is
a special kind of faith healing. The exorcist is the supreme "turner,"
the one who is called upon to wipe the injurious map off the slate, so
that health may be restored. And no matter where this ritual is
practiced, there will always be the same set of actors: the victim, the
exorcist, and the supporting community, lending support to the view
that we are dealing with the same phenomenon no matter what the
faith might be.

In summary, then, we need to understand a number of different
concepts in order to comprehend the worldwide phenomenon of
possession and exorcism. On the psychological level, we have come to
know the notion underlying all possession, namely, that the body is a
shell, inhabited by a soul, and that this shell may on occasion be
surrendered to an intrusive alien entity. The nature of this being and
the circumstances of entry are culturally structured, so culture is
another important basic term. On the physiological level, there is the
altered state of consciousness of ecstasy and the emergence of brain
maps. Ritual acts as a bridge that connects the events on the psychological and the physiological levels, leading to experience. That ties in
with healing, especially in our context with the cure of injurious
possession by the ritual of exorcism.

2 PIRITUALISM

To many people, the idea of possession by an alien entity is a frightening one, because the word conjures up stories of malevolent, demonic intrusion. Actually, though, the experience does not always involve evil spirits. Quite often, instead, the beings in question are kindly, helpful, or, at most, dangerous. As to the reasons why there should be such a variety of traditions about this experience, we have to turn briefly to the history of human cultural evolution.[1]

The whole complex of possession and the rituals concerning it must be quite old, judging from the fact that the tradition is so widely distributed. It is known, for example, to horticulturalists, as we saw with the Yąnomamö (see chap. 1), where the medicine men invited the spirits into their chests. The horticulture of the Yąnomamö Indians is a very ancient form of cultivation, arising directly from the original style of subsistence of all humankind, that of hunting and gathering. It survives to this day as a sophisticated adaptation to tropical rain forests, for instance in South America. Its name derives from the Latin word *hortus,* "garden," because instead of open fields these societies work small, gardenlike plots. The area for the gardens is burned over and yields a harvest only for about three years. That forces horticulturalist societies to be on the move all the time, and their villages are not permanent. Such mobility necessitates a constant close interaction with their surroundings, their natural habitat, which demands flexibility and adaptiveness. Quite logically, their ethical system is also based on appropriateness, for they cannot afford the rigidity of a world view that is based on the cleavage between good and evil. It follows that their spirits are adaptable, too; they are *neither good nor evil,* they are simply powerful. In Japan, the only large modern state with strong ties to horticulturalist tradition, spirits of this nature tend to predominate in possession, as we shall see in chapter 5.

By contrast, our own Western cultural tradition involves a conflict between good and evil, which is associated with a different and later life style, that of the agriculturalists, the tillers of large, open fields. We share this subsistence pattern with a number of other societies, for instance with some African ones, and also with China and India. It represents an adaptation to an ecology usually but not always in the temperate zone that allows the development of large open fields, which retain their fertility for a long time. The settlements of these tillers of the soil are permanent, and neither their homes nor their fields can be abandoned without causing great hardship. In such a situation, as I show in the work referred to above,

> the tiller is in constant conflict with undesirable, "bad" plants, animals, and people that try to intrude into his fields, barns, and village. He has an intense feeling of being protected "within," while trying to keep the "outside," that which is alien and dangerous, both human and alternate-reality agencies, from penetrating.

In agriculturalist tradition, the inside-outside, that is, the good-bad, distinction is transposed also into the hereafter, so that there is a heaven and a hell, and a host of *very good* and *abysmally evil* spirit beings. And since hell is such an undesirable place, evil spirits tend to roam the human world instead, plaguing the people.

In general outline, the agriculturalist tradition was also retained in the cities that began emerging in the course of this agriculturalist "revolution." Why, then, we might ask ourselves, do we have a situation where, as in the case of Spiritualism, evil spirits are no longer recognized? Perhaps the fundamental change that led to this development was the increasing openness of the modern city, which came with the Industrial Revolution. That blurred the "inside-outside," and with it the good-bad, distinction. One sign of this development, at least in the West, was that almost imperceptibly at first, and later at an accelerated pace, the image of Satan as it prevailed in the Middle Ages, of the fallen angel, the ruler of hell, the spirit representing ultimate evil, started to fade. Eventually, Lucifer became a stranger in the modern Western city, an intruder, no longer recognized even if he did possess anybody, so that such a person was then classed not as possessed but as mentally ill. Specifically for nineteenth-century America and Spiritualism, the anthropologist Wolf-Dieter Storl points out,[2]

> An analysis of the ethnic origins of early American Spiritualists indicates that they were predominantly New England Calvinists, who divided the world into good and bad, God and Satan, lost and redeemed on the basis of a simple scheme of black and white. . . . But

after the frontier had been pacified, this strict Calvinism lost its per-
suasiveness. The transcendentalists developed an ideology of op-
timism, which denied the existence of evil and interpreted everything
as positive and progress. (1983:10, 11)

This development coincided with a gradual overall secularization of
life, so that in the view of many, the city became "rational," its
churches turned predominantly into social rather than religious institutions, which were mainly interested in promoting the detachment
of philosophical and theological issues.

Yet when we inspect the life of a modern city, that rather simplistic
view turns out to be biased. The fabric of the urban centers around
the world is not thoroughly gray, not uniformly "rational," turning its
back not only on old-fashioned Satan but also on religious experience
generally. It is shot through instead with cult activities anything but
"rational," and among these cults and religions,[3] those centering on
the experience of possession have by far the greatest number of
adherents. Only the demons have been dispossessed, with the city
turning to helpful, friendly beings of the alternate reality instead.

In this chapter, we will examine a religious innovation of this
character involving possession, namely, Spiritualism, where the possessing entities are disposed kindly toward their human hosts. It
started in an urban ambient among disaffected Protestants and is the
first positive possession cult developed independently in the West.
Subsequently, it served as a source for many ideas in other related
movements.

The roots of modern Spiritualism reach back into the eighteenth
century. The Swedish visionary Emanuel Swedenborg is usually credited with being its philosophical forerunner, although possession by
spirits could not have been further from his mind. He was born in
1688, the son of a Swedish Lutheran bishop, but spent much of his
adult life in England, where his major works were published, and
where he died in 1772. He was what in the parlance of his time was
called a natural philosopher. Highly educated, he was interested in
the natural sciences, in mining, physics, and chemistry, and he wrote
voluminously about these topics. Although quite successful, he was
personally dissatisfied with these pursuits, for, as he wrote, he missed
the "mystery of life." So he turned to anatomy and philosophy.
Clearly, that offered no fulfillment either, for in his fifty-seventh year
he underwent a severe emotional crisis. Its resolution came in an
impressive visionary experience; that is, he spontaneously strayed into
ecstasy:

The same night the world of spirits, hell and heaven, were con-
vincingly opened to me, where I found many persons of my acquaint-

ance of all conditions. Thereafter the Lord daily opened the eyes of my
spirit to see in perfect wakefulness what was going on in the other
world, and to converse, broadawake, with angels and spirits.[4]

Basing himself on this event, Swedenborg argued that one could
know God and the inner reality of things only through "intuitive"
knowledge, that is, knowledge obtained in trance. He retained his
newly found ability for entering into this altered state until the time of
his death, twenty-eight years later. What he saw with his "spiritual
sight" and the theological and philosophical system he developed on
the basis of his visions constituted the topic of his subsequent very
influential writings, which became well known also in this country,
especially through such transcendental writers as Emerson.

Spiritualists credit Swedenborg with being the first one to conceive
of the spirit world as a realm of natural law. In great detail, he
described the celestial spheres as he saw them in his visions. He
developed a doctrine of correspondences, arguing that the spiritual
and the natural world related to each other as cause and effect. The
natural world, he wrote, had a spiritual force behind it, producing
and sustaining it. What is especially remarkable, and which fore-
shadows the exclusive preoccupation of the Spiritualists with the spirits of the dead, is the fact that he saw "many persons of my
acquaintance," that is, the souls of the departed, as soon as he first
caught sight of those celestial ranges. In fact, all the beings he encountered there, both angels and devils, were to him of the same order as
humans, having lived on the earth before. The devils were simply
underdeveloped souls, the angels highly developed ones. In other
words, the six celestial spheres he perceived were populated exclusively by the spirits of the dead, all good, even if some more so than
others. The only concession to traditional theology was his admission
that three of the six spheres constituted hell. But no one was ever sent
there; its denizens were simply "attracted" to it because of some
inherent mean streak. Anyone could eventually progress out of that
inhospitable region.

The reason there is no bust to Emanuel Swedenborg in any Spiritualist church today is that, understandably, he could not totally
shake off the system of thought that had shaped him in the house of
his father—who, after all, was a Lutheran clergyman. As if atoning for
his unconventional insights in the matter of hell and the devils, he
interpreted all his other visions in terms of orthodox Protestant theology, which was to become anathema to the later Spiritualists. And
not many Spiritualists realize that he was the one who started to give
new and unexpected interpretations to key words of the Bible. In this,
he pointed the way to modern Spiritualists, who have a kind of

"newspeak," where they apply words of everyday usage to communicate secret meanings. As the anthropologist Irving I. Zaretsky has shown, that shelters them from unwelcome intruders.[5] Swedenborg was important to Spiritualism as a pathfinder. But its theological foundations were created by a far more independent soul than the Swedish visionary, an American frontiersman by the name of Andrew Jackson Davis.

Andrew Jackson Davis was born in Blooming Grove, New York, in 1826, the son of a poor leatherworker. He was a sickly child and did poorly in the few grades he attended in school. But when out in the fields by himself, the boy heard comforting voices, and when his mother died, he saw a vision of a lovely home in a land of brightness, which was, he was sure, where his mother now lived. Had he been born to a family of hunters and herders in Siberia, there would have been great rejoicing over such a child, for those experiences are among the signs exhibited by a future shaman. In the rough and tumble of the American frontier, they were hardly among the qualities parents most desired in their sons. In fact, young Davis's prospects for a satisfying future would have been quite dismal, had it not been for the visit to the village of a traveling showman, who made his living by exhibiting the wonders of mesmerism.

Franz Anton Mesmer (1733–1815), who gave his name to mesmerism, the early term for hypnotism, was an Austrian physician who believed that the planets emanated a fluid that humans attracted the way a magnet attracted iron nails. He called this supposed fluid "animal magnetism" and thought that humans could collect it in themselves. After concentrating enough of this fluid in himself, a "magnetizer" could then transfer it to a patient and thus produce a cure. What is important about Mesmer is the fact that he did not just formulate a theory, he actually tried it, and in doing so, he developed the prototype of the modern Spiritualist séance. As J. Stillson Judah describes it,

> A number of people sat around a tub . . . containing supposedly magnetized material. Each held his neighbor's hand as well as a rod extending from the tub, while waiting expectantly to be magnetized, i.e., hypnotized and cured of his ailment. (1967:51)

Mesmer set the trend for such experimentation, which for a while became all the rage in the parlors of Europe. Neither was it restricted to interested dilettantes. As early as 1787, Swedenborg's Société Exegétique et Philanthropique of Stockholm reported on experiments using Mesmer's method; however, apparently they were done not for purposes of healing but in order to establish communication with the spirits of the dead. In the séances of the society, these spirits allegedly spoke through a young woman. Magnetists proliferated in Germany and England, publishing a spate of books about contacts with spirits, reporting clairvoyant powers for diagnosing ailments, and prescribing remedies. Especially the latter claims prompted the Medical Section of the Paris Royal Academy in 1825 to carry out its own investigations and to attest to the validity of the kind of trance mesmerism produced and its therapeutic value.

For the young boys in a backwoods village in New York State, letting themselves be hypnotized by a traveling carnival entertainer was, of course, just another game. But for Andrew Jackson Davis, it took the place of a shamanistic initiation. He showed astounding aptitude, being able in trance to read letters with his eyes bandaged, and seeing the inside of unfamiliar houses, or of a person's body with all organs standing out in a bright glow. In addition, it was soon found, as Sir Arthur Conan Doyle tells in his history of Spiritualism, that

> his soul or etheric body could be liberated by the magnetic manipulation of his employer, and could be sent forth like a carrier pigeon with the certainty that it would come home again bearing any desired information. Apart from the humanitarian mission on which it was usually engaged it would sometimes roam at will, and he has described in wonderful passages how he would see a translucent earth beneath him, with the great veins of mineral beds shining through like masses of molten metal, each with its own fiery radiance. (1926:I,44–45)

As anyone with even a passing acquaintance with the literature on shamanism, such as the works of Mircea Eliade, will immediately note, that is an accurate description of a spirit journey. The following experience of Davis is equally well known to shamans, especially from initiation:

> On the evening of March 6, 1844, Davis was suddenly possessed by some power which led him to fly from the little town of Poughkeepsie, where he lived, and to hurry off, in a condition of semitrance, upon a rapid journey. When he regained his clear perception he found himself among wild mountains, and there he claims to have met two venerable men with whom he held intimate and elevating communion, the one upon medicine and the other upon morals. All night he was out, and when he inquired his whereabouts next morning he was told that he was in the Catskill Mountains and forty miles from his home. (1926:I,45)

Later he was to claim that one of those advisers had been Galen, the famous Greek physician of classical antiquity. He received a magic staff from him, with which he was able to learn about various diseases and their cures. Galen also taught him that disease had no effect on the interior spiritual essence of a person, which could be mobilized in healing. The second personage, Davis maintained, had been Swedenborg, who offered to become his guide.

It is curious, of course, that hypnotic manipulation should induce such clearly shamanistic experiences in Davis. Anthropological fieldwork has not identified hypnosis as we know it in the West as an induction strategy for ecstasy in non-Western religious communities. The switch becomes intelligible, however, if we consider how the ordinary state of consciousness and the altered ones relate to each other. We might think of the ordinary state of perception as a building that is our home for most of our waking hours. It surrounds us, protects us, but also confines us. This solid building does not even seem to have any windows, so that the illusion arises that there is nothing beyond its walls. That is not the case, however. We regularly escape when we dream, to what we might think of as another building next door, which is equally ours. It contains a number of separate rooms, of which that of our dreams is only one. The door to the dream room is sleep: we cannot dream unless we sleep. There are also rooms of daydreaming, the hypnotic state, the various meditative states, ecstasy, and many other hitherto unidentified changes of consciousness, each one with its own door of the physical changes necessary to enter it. There may be some resistance when we want to get into the second building, its front door may be heavy, but once inside, it is relatively easy to pass from room to room. Professor Appel of Brandeis University, who did anthropological fieldwork in Indonesia, told me that experienced mediums there could easily slip from sleep directly into the ecstatic state. The same transition can inadvertently happen between the hypnotic state and ecstasy. A psychologist once sent me a tape for analysis, where a young woman in hypnotic regression spoke of her adventures with Martians. Suddenly, as she recalled her arms becoming stiff during that encounter, she slipped into the typical intonation pattern of glossolalia described in chapter 1. With the use of the level recorder, an instrument used in the phonetics lab that registers changes in the pressure density of intonation, it was easy to see the difference between the flat, irregular curves of her hypnotic speech and those of her glossolalia with their clear, relatively high peaks at the end of the first third of each utterance unit. In Davis's case, his nervous system was already familiar with ecstasy, and so it was natural for it to follow that corridor once he found himself inside the right building. Soon after dictating his book (see below), according to Doyle before he was twenty-one, he was able to dispense with the help of a hypnotist and could enter into the religious trance state on his own.

Given Davis's special gifts, he did not long continue as a carnival attraction. For a while, he served a kind of trance apprenticeship with a local tailor who acted as his hypnotist, and for whose clients he diagnosed illnesses and prescribed remedies. He was then befriended by a physician, a Dr. Lyon. For some time he had been wanting to put his experiences and insights into a book. He was only nineteen when with the help of Dr. Lyon, this dream became a reality. Dr. Lyon took his protégé to New York, where they recruited a clergyman, the Reverend William Fishbough, to act as a scribe. It must have been quite a sensation when for two years, day after day and often in the presence of hundreds of spectators, Lyon hypnotized young Davis, who would then, drawing on the inspiration of the intensely creative religious trance state, dictate his *Nature's Divine Revelations: The Principles of Nature, her Divine Revelations, and a Voice to Mankind*. The work, which was heralded as providing "a first clear description of the spirit world and its spheres," unencumbered by "the preconceptions and misconceptions of orthodox theology,"[6] was an instant success.

Why Davis's book would become so popular is not difficult to understand: it appeared at the right time and in the right place. Davis was born in a period of considerable social unrest on the frontier in the western part of the state of New York. His natal region, dubbed the "burned-over district,"[7] gave rise to a great deal of utopian experimentation. Communes of the Fourierists, the Owenites, and the Transcendentalists flourished in the area. That was where the temperance movement started, and the anti-Masonic movement. New sects sprang up like mushrooms after a spring rain: several Swedenborgian sects, the sects of the Mormons (1823), of the Shakers (1830), of the Adventists and the Millerites (1844), all hailed from that part of the state and arose within the same few decades. Davis created a synthesis of the thoughts current in his environment, of ideas from Swedenborg, freemasonry, and Neoplatonism, and material from European folklore. That is, he formulated much that those dissatisfied with traditional Calvinist doctrine could identify with. He was, as the anthropologist Peter Worsley[8] defines the term, a "charismatic" figure for his age, one who found effective expression for what everyone had on his mind. In addition, quite a number of the new sects, the Swedenborgians, the Mormons, and the Shakers, started out as the result of an ecstatic experience of their founder, and the Shakers institutionalized ecstatic trance behavior. And last but not least, Davis's views and experiences fitted in with the urgent desire of the age to be able to find so-called scientific proof for the existence of the world of the spirits. So actually, since he had not been destined to be a shaman child, the next best thing that could have happened to him was to be born in this part of the world and into this era.

That this man, then, America's first metaphysical philosopher, should become permanently associated with Spiritualism, is a matter of affinity of thought. But we cannot underestimate the role of historical coincident, either: his first book came out in 1847, just one year before the famous Fox sisters began hearing the spirit rappings in Hydesville.

Hydesville was at the beginning of the last century a farming community near Rochester, New York. The log cabin that the Fox family moved into in December of 1847 was known as a haunted house, but it was not until March 1848 that the family experienced the rappings that had all the earmarks of a poltergeist phenomenon. The latter is often associated with teenage children, and the family had two daughters living at home, both early teenagers, the older Margaret and the younger Kate. What the family heard that night was a knocking, together with noises of furniture moving. The disturbance persisted during the following nights and became quite frightening. Poltergeist experiences are not rare, but what sets this incident off from others is that one night it occurred to Kate, the younger girl, to challenge what seemed an independently existing entity acting up and interfering with their rest to repeat the snaps of her fingers. The challenge was instantly accepted, with every snap answered by a corresponding knock. This happened even if Kate produced no sound, only the movement, leading everyone to assume that the invisible partner could not just hear but also see. As a next move, Kate and her sister created a code, asking for two raps for yes and one for no. Intrigued, their mother got into the act and started asking questions about her own past, which to her surprise were answered with remarkable accuracy. As to the rapper's own identity, the spirit professed to be the ghost of a peddler, murdered in the cabin, with robbery as the motive. Subsequently, skeletal remains were indeed found, though not at the spot in the basement indicated by the rapping conversationalist. Although the existence of the peddler, whose name had been tapped out, could never be documented, the adventures of the Fox sisters were considered scientific proof of the factual existence of spirits, and the possibility of a rather simple strategy for receiving answers from the beyond became the talk of the town.

As could be expected, the New York newspapers gave the events in Hydesville coverage under banner headlines, turning the matter into a sensation. It will be recalled that contacts with the spirit world had been reported before, from Stockholm, from France and Germany, but it took the very special social and intellectual circumstances around New York to create what amounted to an outbreak of a mass trance movement, attributed by at least one author, namely, Doyle, to an outside power having rather remarkable properties:

It should be stated that either this power was contagious or else it was descending upon many individuals independently from some common source. . . . It was like some psychic cloud descending from on high and showing itself on those who were susceptible. (1926:I,77)

The trance phenomena began cropping up in an even larger area when the two Fox girls went to live with relatives in Rochester, and the mysterious rapping went along with them. That indicated to everyone captivated by the goings-on that the spirits were not tied to a particular building. The news encouraged enthusiastic experimentation, and to the delight of everyone concerned, many different spirits, all of them of the dear departed, began emerging. As Doyle relates,

> The whole course of the movement now had widened and taken a more important turn. It was no longer a murdered man calling for justice. The pedlar seemed to have been used as a pioneer, and now that he had found the opening and the method, a myriad of intelligences were swarming at his back. . . . The intelligent knockings purported to be from the deceased friends of those inquirers who were prepared to take a serious interest in the matter and to gather in reverent mood to receive the messages. That they still lived and still loved was the constant message from the beyond, accompanied by many material tests, which confirmed the wavering faith of the new adherents of the movement. (1926:I,79)

The question that clearly suggests itself at this point is, why this exclusive preoccupation with the spirits of the dead, already adumbrated in Swedenborg's writings? Traditionally, ghosts are feared. Among *vodun* adherents, serious illness is interpreted as being due to possession by the spirits of the dead. Non-Western societies have elaborate burial rites, which are aimed at making sure that the spirits of the departed understand that the way back to the world of the living is blocked. "Forget us!" they are told in a Tewa Indian prayer. Such spirits may perhaps be invited back once in a while for a brief communitywide celebration, as it used to be during Halloween or All Souls' Day. But if they need to be feted, as among some Indian societies of the American Northwest, they are still not allowed to possess the members of their former families. It is the invited guests that can, without suffering harm, receive them and, by eating the festive food, share it with the spirits.

To understand the turn toward these once-feared spirit entities, we need to remember once more the Calvinist roots of Spiritualism. Spirits of saints, which play an important role in Umbanda (see chap. 3), were no longer part of the belief system, and with evil spirits also excluded, the spirits of the dead were the only ones left. That has remained true in this country even in contexts having nothing to do with Spiritualism or other kinds of possession. It is borne out, for example, by the reader reports published in "True Mystic Experiences," a regular feature in the popular magazine *Fate,* and by reports of those who have had a near-death experience.[9] Invariably, they encounter close relatives or beloved friends, that is, spirits of the dead, on the other side. The anthropologist Irving I. Zaretsky, who did fieldwork in Spiritualist churches in California in the 1970s, offers the following explanation:

> Many of the nuclear groups [of the Spiritualist churches] are middle-aged men and women who never married or are divorced or widowed. Often they live in apartments in large downtown complexes or sometimes in hotels catering to permanent residents. . . . They work at white collar jobs, secretarial, semi-skilled or semi-professional. Their free time is largely unoccupied. They spend much of that free time seeking companionship. . . . Church participants speak about and communicate through their behavior an intense sense of individual loneliness. Even those who are married or have a steady companion relate to the church as individuals rather than as couples. Most adherents are looking to fill an empty social space in their life. . . . In searching for help in decision-making, these individuals turn to Spiritualist churches and to the realm of the spirits who are often the departed relatives or friends of the individual. Such spirits can be relied on for good advice and are also regarded as substitutes for the social vacancies individuals feel in their life. (1974:170–71)

In the course of its history, Spiritualism has, as could be expected, not remained isolated from other traditions concerning spirits and having currency in the larger society. The folklorist Linda Dégh (personal communication) tells of the activity of a self-proclaimed Spiritualist exorcist who cleanses cemeteries, houses, and persons of the injurious effects of the presence of spirits of dead relatives. According to some Spiritualists, the spirits of their unborn children or their guardian angels may act as spirit guides, and Indian spirits are frequently mentioned. The latter feature is thought by some observers to represent a borrowing from the religions of the Plains Indians. But there was little interest in or knowledge of those religions in the nineteenth century. Others argue, and this may be closer to the truth, that to the American, the Indian is a figure shrouded in mystery, a guide to the unknown paths of the spirit world, to which he has a special relationship as a member of a "dying race."[10] In the early period of Spiritualism, Davis provided important details about the nature of the spirits of the dead, which became basic to the new movement. Thus, in the first volume of his *Great Harmonia,* he describes a death scene. Quoting Doyle:

He sat by a dying woman and observed every detail of the soul's
departure. . . . He then tells how, having first thrown himself into what
he calls the "Superior condition," he thus observed the stages from the
spiritual side. "The material eye can only see what is material, and the
spiritual what is spiritual," but as everything would seem to have a
spiritual counterpart the result is the same. Thus when a spirit comes
to us it is not us that it perceives but our etheric bodies, which are,
however, duplicates of our real ones.

It was this etheric body which Davis saw emerging from its poor
outworn envelope of protoplasm. . . . The process began by an extreme concentration in the brain, which became more and more luminous as the extremities became darker. . . . Then the new body begins
to emerge, the head disengaging itself first. Soon it has completely
freed itself, standing at right angles to the corpse, with its feet near the
head and with some luminous vital band between which corresponds
to the umbilical cord. When the cord snaps a small portion is drawn
back into the dead body and it is this which preserves it from instant
putrefaction. As to the etheric body, it takes some little time to adapt
itself to its new surroundings, and in this instance it then passed out
through the open doors. "I saw her pass through the adjoining room,
out of the door and step from the house into the atmosphere. . . .
Immediately after her emergement from the house she was joined by
two friendly spirits from the spiritual country, and after tenderly
recognising and communing with each other the three, in the most
graceful manner, began ascending obliquely through the ethereal en-
velopment of our globe. They walked so naturally and fraternally
together that I could scarcely realise the fact that they trod the air—
they seemed to be walking on the side of a glorious but familiar
mountain. I continued to gaze upon them until the distance shut them
from my view." (1926:I, 49–51)

As is evident in this example, Davis steers clear of Christian imagery. Quite generally, he rejected Christianity even in its most liberal
form, trusting his own visionary insights instead. God was revealed to
him as the "Divine Mind," not in the Bible but in the universe as he
experienced it. As a man living in the era of early industrialization, he
in addition propounded that progress to ever greater perfection was a
law of nature, also effective on the spiritual plane. Its spheres were
governed by harmony, and humans needed to be part of it. This
"harmonial philosophy" is the central theme of his world view, and it
became basic to early Spiritualism.

Davis was associated with Spiritualism also in practical ways. He
participated in the founding of Harmonial City, a Spiritualist colony
at Kiantone Valley near Jamestown, New York, which was active from
1850 to 1858. He remained their principal apologist until his death in
1910, and his influence was still felt a generation later. In 1931, the
General Assembly of Spiritualists of New York adopted the following

resolution (Lawton 1932:2): "We accept as the fundamentals of Spiritualism the philosophy of the Divine Harmony of Nature as expressed by Andrew Jackson Davis."

Yet we detect a certain ambivalence in the attitude of modern Spiritualism toward Davis. His statements are quoted frequently, yet his works are rarely read and are not stocked in Spiritualist churches. Only the Library of Congress possesses a complete set. The reason is that Davis preferred "to commune with the Divine Mind" to spirit possession. Psychologically and from the point of view of brain organization, that is entirely understandable. As pointed out before, Davis's religious trance experiences concentrated on visions and spirit journeys. He was not geared to possession. And so he considered it unnecessary to keep contacting the dead on a regular basis. However, it was this experience that in the development of Spiritualism until the present remained central for the movement, and so Andrew Jackson Davis faded into the background.

Although no longer the sensation that it used to be in its early period, Spiritualism is still a viable religion today, claiming, according to some sources, about one million adherents nationwide. Theologically, it does not sponsor a uniform and codified body of beliefs. However, most adherents subscribe to a tripartite view of humans: a human being consists of a material body; it contains an immaterial indestructible spirit, the carrier and preserver of personal and human values through eternity; and this spirit in turn has a body, the soul or soul body.

The individual churches have no paying membership, and each church is shaped by the personality of its pastor. It is hierarchically organized, with the core group usually closely linked to the pastor by family or friendship ties. As Linda Dégh observed (personal communication), in American towns these core groups appear like extended families, with especially the women having extensive social contacts. The services include sermons, healing, and, as the central ritual, the providing of messages by the mediums. These mediums are usually women. They are trained in special courses, mainly in visualization. Lawton quotes the well-known spiritualist Arthur Ford, whose development classes he attended in Lily Dale, New York, in 1929:

> In order to develop your mediumistic powers, you must learn to visualize. This is not difficult. . . . Close your eyes, bring up the picture of some loved one whose face you know very well. Start by trying to see the spirit you know best, your mother or brother or sister, because you have known them all your life. Such visualizations occur and spirits come just before you fall asleep at night or when you are waking up in the morning, but they stay only a moment. If you want them to stay

longer, breathe deeply and slowly and hold your breath, and the spirit will stay. When you gasp in surprise you expell your breath and lose the picture. . . . Draw in your breath and the picture is held, and as you hold it, the picture comes closer and clearer. (1932:359)

Besides giving lectures in such development classes, Ford also demonstrated the transmission of messages, as it is customary in church services or private séances:

I get the name . . . of . . . Schleming.
Here.
Lucy comes to me. It seems she was a friend of yours—a sweetheart, because I see you close together. She died in an accident on the 13th of February.
13th of January.
13th of January, yes. It was an automobile accident.
Yes.
You were with her.
Yes.
She tells me to tell you that she heard you, even though she could not answer. You picked her up and you held her in your arms and said, "It's Bill, Lucy, answer me, just one word!" Isn't that so?
Yes, every word.
She tells me to say that she is waiting for you, that though you could not marry, she is your wife and will join you when you come over. She was buried in a little hill in Hackensack.
It was a hillock all right, but not in Hackensack—in Nyack.
I knew it was in New Jersey. You came and put flowers on her grave, March 22nd, and you came up here to communicate with her.
Yes.
You almost ran off the road coming here, right into a ditch.
Yes.
She tells me she was at the steering wheel and helped you right the car, otherwise you would have turned over and landed in the ditch. She is always helping you. You menioned her name at the time, whispering, "Lucy, dear." (1932:365–66)

For later development, Ford recommended a home circle of seven or eight participants, sitting regularly once or twice a week for six months. Spiritualists contend that anyone can be trained to be a medium, but as in everything else, outstanding performance is the result not only of training but of exceptional personal gifts, as well. Doyle quotes a letter of a Mr. Livermore, a New York banker. This man recommends Kate Fox, who had developed into an accomplished medium in adulthood, to a friend in England:

> Miss Fox, taken all in all, is no doubt the most wonderful living medium. . . . The communications through her are very remarkable, and have come to me frequently from my wife (Estelle), in perfect idiomatic French, and sometimes in Spanish and Italian, whilst she herself is not acquainted with any of these languages. (1926:I, 95)

Using the concept of the brain maps as developed by Putnam and Pitblado, we might speculate that the following process takes place during the training for mediumship. The special breathing techniques and concentration, together with cultural expectation, make it possible for the medium to enter the religious trance; being trained in visualizing departed spirits then enables the medium temporarily to switch off her own map, making room for another, alien one, namely, that of the possessing spirit. At the dissolution of the trance, the medium's own map once more takes over. In a light religious trance, like the one into which mediums usually switch during a routine public service, the map of the possessing spirit may be no more substantial than a passing shadow. Practiced and highly gifted mediums can command clearer and more impressive spirit maps.

In this context, Ford makes an intriguing remark in the development class that Lawton attended, which provides some additional insight into the nature and stability of these maps. He says that "spirits that come often, come better." That would mean that a repeated calling forth of the same alien map makes it more distinct. Yet the new map is still not as stable as that of the medium's own personality, for he continues with the observation, "But after they [the spirits] have been over a long time they have difficulty in giving messages, they forget" (1932:359). In other words, there is a tendency after a while for these acquired maps to dissolve permanently. Unfortunately, we do not learn about the span of time involved.

Whether all these assumptions agree with what actually happens, we will not know until further laboratory research. The self-reporting of mediums is of little help here, for we should remember that they are as little aware of the neurophysiological events that take place during possession as we are of what happens in the brain when we see an object or hear a piece of music.

In addition to giving messages, the mediums are also healers, performing this task both in public services and in private séances and individual consultations. Andrew Jackson Davis pointed the movement early in this direction when he told about his meeting in a vision with Galen, of classical Greek fame. When in the course of his fieldwork Lawton visited the Spiritualist camp at Lily Dale, New York, in 1929, he encountered a pronounced "clinical" atmosphere because of the presence of the aged and the ailing in search of help. Yet there were no physicians or even a drugstore in Lily Dale, for cures were expected from spirit sources alone. These attitudes and the basic principles of Spiritualist curing are well illustrated by the definition of healing adopted by the National Spiritualist Association at its 1909 convention in Rochester, New York:

> 1. It is the sense of this convention that Spiritual Healing is a gift possessed by certain Spiritualist mediums, and that this gift is exercised by and through the direction and influence of excarnate spiritual beings for the relief, cure and healing of both mental and physical diseases of human kind; and that the results of spiritual healing are produced in several ways, to wit:
> (a) By the spiritual influences working through the body of the medium and thus infusing curative, stimulating and vitalizing fluids and energy into the diseased parts of the patients body.
> (b) By the spiritual influences illuminating the brain of the healing mediums and thereby intensifying the perception of the medium so that the cause, nature and seat of the disease in the patient becomes known to the medium; and the herb or other remedy which will benefit the patient also becomes known to the medium.
> (c) Through the application of above treatments whereby spiritual beings combine their own healing forces with the magnetism and vitalizing energy of the mediums and convey them to the patient who is distant from the medium and cause them to be absorbed by the system of the patient.[11]

In the course of time, Spiritualist thought and experiences spread well beyond the confines of the churches and the séances. The description, for instance, that Davis gives of the soul of a departed being joined upon emergence from the body by two spirits and guided up into the clouds, has become a standard fixture of Hollywood movies. In a recent television advertisement, the startled victim of a fatal car crash is escorted up into the clouds by two solicitous male figures in snow-white suits. Their friendly explanation makes clear that it would be wise to buy life insurance before one is unexpectedly called to the beyond. The Spiritualist's astral body, the aura, and the spirit guide have become part of the language. Ascended masters give instruction and advice through mediums, with the activity now called "channeling." They are often "Tibetans," such as the one consulted at the Tibetan Foundation in Youngtown, Arizona; or at least extremely old (35,000 years!), such as the newly famous Ramtha, the spirit guide of a California businesswoman. Extraterrestrials have entered the scene. They are experienced as teachers, as in the case of the "UFO prophet," Ted Owens, or as possessing beings, as I was told by an Appalachian consultant. This young woman maintained that a number of her friends were not at all what they seemed. They were in reality simply shells possessed by wise, kindly, and powerful aliens, sent to earth to give advice.

Neither did Spiritualism remain confined to the English-speaking world. It has adherents in all the Western countries, changing emphasis in the process of propagation, but not losing its essential orientation. In Mexico, for instance, Spiritualism is not a middle-class religion with a primarily white clientele. Neither is it principally sought out in order to contact departed family members. People usually have access to effective extended families even in the cities. Besides, there is by tradition quite a bit of fear attached to family ghosts. Instead, Mexican Spiritualism is a vigorous health-care system, which has a long history and is still growing. As such, it cuts across ethnic, religious, and class lines, and its mediums are healers, being possessed by long-dead physicians, often bearing Indian names.[12]

In our next chapter, we will come to know such a complex system of health care and personal counseling, which plays an important role in Latin America and boasts of millions of followers, namely, *Umbanda,* a Brazilian mediumistic healing cult. It has incorporated some elements of Spiritualism, but as we shall see, it is actually an amalgam of a number of disparate traditions and is well on its way to becoming the leading Brazilian religion.

3 HEALING IN UMBANDA

Continuing with our review of positive spirit possession, we want to treat Umbanda next. This Brazilian religion has a complex history, with its roots reaching back into Africa, Europe, and Indian America. The sugar plantations in the northeastern part of Brazil employed African slaves in the sixteenth century. They brought with them their own religious observances from Dahomey, the Congo, and Angola. They also carried along the Yoruba tradition, a syncretic form of which evolved into Haitian *vodun,* which we touched on in chapter 1. Gradually, beliefs concerning the Catholic saints of the plantation owners and the African gods began to overlap; they became syncretized. When in 1888 the slaves were emancipated in Brazil, they began moving south, into the cities that offered jobs in their developing industries. Once there, the Afro-Brazilians started cult centers for the practice of their various religions. These were already syncretic, some even incorporating American Indian traits. But they varied according to which of the African traditions was predominant.

Garbled and sensationalized reports had appeared for years in the Western press about these various cults, especially about Umbanda, which rose to prominence after the middle of this century. Serious research by behavioral scientists is relatively recent, however. The present discussion is based on the work of two investigators, Esther J. Pressel,[1] an American anthropologist who studied Umbanda in São Paulo in 1967, and a German psychologist, Horst H. Figge,[2] who lived in Brazil for seven years and did participant observation in Umbanda centers from April 1969 to June 1970 in Rio de Janeiro. He also spent time in such centers in Salvador, Bahía, and Recife, Pernambuco.

In popular reports, Umbanda has often been confused with Macumba, which combines Yoruba, Congolese, and Angolan traits. Actually, Macumba is thought to be the immediate predecessor to Umbanda and has today been supplanted by it. In addition to African gods and ritual, the following Macumba traits were incorporated into Umbanda:

a. men as well as women can become mediums;

b. lack of group cohesion within the centers because of the urban, fragmented nature of the large industrial cities, mainly São Paulo and Rio de Janeiro.

c. the possessing entities or beings are spirits of the dead; however, for the most part these are nonhistorical characters, dead Afro-Brazilians and American Indians and not spirits of recently dead relatives.

One important feature of Macumba did not become part of Umbanda, and that is black magic. When performing black magic, Macumba practitioners used to work with spirits of people who had led exceptionally wicked lives. Umbanda performs only "white magic," that is, rituals imbued with light, benefiting clients positively and sometimes even the possessing spirit. Black magic became the domain of Quimbanda, a minor cult, where it is used against business competition and in nefarious affairs of the heart.

Umbanda is not exclusively African with some Catholic traits, however. It was also influenced by Spiritualism—coming not from the English-speaking world, though, but from France. French "spiritisme" is a creation of Léon Hipolit Denizart Rivail, better known as Allan Kardec. This French writer became converted to Spiritualism in 1862. Using communications he received through various mediums, he wrote a work that became known in America as *The Spirits' Book* (1875). His teachings about spirits waiting to be helped and especially about reincarnation created quite a split in American Spiritualism for a while. But he became even more influential in South America. In 1957, for instance, the Brazilian government issued a stamp commemorating the "First Centenary of Organized Spiritism," which bears his portrait. Even today, "Kardecismo" is practiced as an independent religion in Brazil.

In São Paulo, Pressel encountered Umbanda and Kardecism more or less mixed, with sometimes the African element predominating, sometimes spiritism; there were centers where the influence of Kardecism was quite minimal, or others where the spirits appeared as African gods but had characteristics found in Kardecism. Figge contends that such transitional forms are characteristic only for São Paulo. He found in Umbanda centers on the Ilha do Governador (Rio de Janeiro) that some of them would set aside certain days for Kardecism sessions, where esoteric "work" was carried out with such spirits. In Kardecism, the spirits possessing the mediums do not provide help; they are the clients of the mediums, as it were. The mediums sit around a table during a séance, and the spirits communicate either through writing or by speaking. The spirits, often of dead lawyers, doctors, kings, or even priests, are, for instance, instructed to acknowledge that they had done wrong during their earthly existence and are made to say certain prayers, or they are taught how to free themselves from earthly desires now that they have passed over. Such activities are kept strictly separate from "pure" Umbanda ritual and belief in the Rio Umbanda centers.

The qualitative difference between Kardec-type spiritism and Umbanda becomes quite clear when we hear what Figge was told by a spirit possessing the leader of a Rio center when he asked what Umbanda was:

> Umbanda is religion; Umbanda is magic; Umbanda is love of neighbor and willingness to sacrifice, gaiety, drums and dance, beautiful dresses and carnival—why not? Umbanda is Africa; Umbanda is Catholicism; Umbanda is Brazil. (Jacket quote)

Very succinctly, this statement attributed to a spirit summarizes the essence of Umbanda as it is practiced today. It is set apart from the ordinary because of its direct contact with beings of the alternate reality, in that sense being religion and magic, two concepts that overlap in all religions. It provides a community for those feeling lost and alienated in the city. The sessions are festive and colorful. Umbanda has roots in Africa. It coexists with Catholicism, with large numbers of Catholics, for instance, getting baptized and married in both a Catholic and an Umbanda ceremony. And adherents of Umbanda are proud of their religion, which they consider quintessentially Brazilian. Finally, the fact that this is a statement by a spirit possessing a cult leader emphasizes the principal attraction of Umbanda, namely, that through its mediums the spirits offer aid and counsel to its adherents.

As demonstrated by the relationship to Kardecism, Umbandists have great latitude in doctrinal matters. Each center reflects not some directives from a central authority but the attitudes of its cult leader; the latter's spirit is considered to be in charge of the center. In fact, Umbanda has no single national organization, and no paying membership, either. Visitors seeking help at the centers may, but are not obligated to, make a monetary contribution. Each center has a number of stable core groups, but the general clientele is shifting, wandering from center to center as personal needs dictate. Clients are recruited from the second-generation, upwardly mobile lower class and the middle class. These are the people who are caught in the rapid social change caused by industrialization, who have lost the protective cohesion of the extended family, and are subject to anxiety, stress, and a host of illnesses, many of them psychosomatic, without a readily available and affordable health-care system. How the Umbanda centers meet the needs of this section of Brazilian society can be understood from a review of the spirits giving aid and advice at the centers.

Caboclos (ca'boklos). *Caboclos* are spirits of dead Indians, proud and self-assured, stern and aloof, lovers of the hunt and good herbalists; they are often generalized into figures of middle age, authoritative and confident. *Caboclos* are consulted in situations requiring quick and decisive action, such as when obtaining or maintaining a job, but also in cases of personal emergency. Pressel relates the following experience recorded early in her fieldwork:

> One of my older informants, Cecilia, took me to the apartment of two young men, insisting that they would be of great use in my work, since they "knew" English. Stepping out of the bus in front of their building, she assured me that I could visit them at any time. I responded that a Brazilian friend in the United States had forewarned me about gossip that would result from going alone to the apartments of men. As we rode up the elevator, Cecilia told me not to worry about this. In about an hour, I learned what she meant. Cecilia's Indian spirit possessed her in an impromptu session. When the major item of spiritual business had been completed, the Indian spirit turned to the men and asked who I was. They introduced me to Cecilia's possessing spirit and explained why I had come to Brazil. The Indian gave his personal blessing to my work and told the others in the room that they should aid my research in any way they could. Furthermore, I was to visit the men and that "nothing" was to happen. Sometime later in the year, when other friends of Cecilia's commented on my visits to the apartment of these men, Cecilia very quickly assured them that her Indian spirit had made the appropriate arrangements for these very proper meetings. (1974:118)

Prêtos velhos (pretos 'velyos).

Prêtos velhos are spirits of dead Afro-Brazilian slaves, very gentle and easy to approach, grandfatherly in manner. They are adept at handling intricate personal problems. They are also fine herbalists and are consulted in cases of illness.

Crianças (cri'ansas).

Crianças are spirits of children that died between the ages of three and five. They can be asked for help in any kind of personal problem, including health.

These three categories of spirits are thought to have passed into

heaven upon death and thus are imbued with "light." There are
others, however, who led wicked lives and therefore have considerably diminished light. These are the *exus* ('ashoos) and their female
counterparts, the *pomba giras* ('pomba 'heras). Suicides automatically
become *exus*, and frequently, at least in São Paulo, they are foreigners.
These *exu* spirits, "without whom nothing can be accomplished," seem
to be more African in character than the others. Although often
represented as demons in the Christian sense, they actually combine
the qualities both of the demonic in the sense of evil and of the spirits
of the evil dead. They are certainly not evil in the absolute sense, and
instead of the satanic they recall North African generative power,
neither good nor evil but rather dangerous. A friendly *exu* can be of
great help, but if it is angered, tangling with it can lead to disaster.
Exus desire light, so will appreciate a candle as a sacrificial offering,
for instance, but if humans refuse to help them, they may cause
suffering. Every medium has his or her own *exu*, yet must continually
be on guard so as not to accede too much to its wishes, for otherwise
the *exu* may take over to the exclusion of everything else. *Exus* can be
prevailed on to crush business competition. Their counterpart, the
good *exus*, who are more evolved spiritually, can help to undo such
machinations. They are the only spirits that demand payment for
their services.

   Exu sessions are accorded great religious significance, because they
afford the opportunity to the *exus* of possessing the mediums and thus
gaining in light. If favored this way, *exus* will be less likely to appear
uninvited, disrupting sessions with other spirits. Even externally,
these session are set off from others, with the cult leader and also
many mediums exchanging their white and lacy garments for a bright
red skirt and black blouse.

Orixás ('orishas).

   While the syncretization between the *exu* spirits and devils remained
quite superficial, it was more thoroughgoing with regard to the *orixás*,
which are not ordinary spirits like the preceding ones. They are
instead Yoruba gods who were identified with Catholic saints during
the period of slavery. That this process may have been more surface
than substance is indicated by Figge's observation that it is usually the
outsider who thinks that the saint's name and that of an *orixá* are
synonymous. Among cult leaders, the prevailing opinion seems to be
that they designate two distinct entities. Supposedly, each saint, just
like any person or spirit of the dead, has an *orixá*, but is not identical
with it. Some especially popular saints are believed to have been
favored by an *orixá* or might even have been that *orixá*'s medium.
Interestingly, that makes the *orixás*, that is, Yoruba gods, superior in

rank to the European saints. Apparently, *orixás* can possess mediums in Rio, while this possibility is expressly denied by Pressel for mediums in São Paulo. But in both cities they have important roles as guardian spirits. For a fee, the cult leader will carry out the necessary divination for an individual to discover which *orixá* protects him.

In the divine hierarchy of Umbanda, God as the supreme ruler is named but distant. Umbandists do not consider themselves outside of Catholicism, but feel that the place for divine worship is the church, not the Umbanda center. The statue of the Virgin Mary, however, *Nossa Senhora Aparecida* ("Our Lady Who Appeared"), a replica of a wood carving found by fishermen in 1717 and credited with many miracles, can be found on the altars of countless Umbanda centers.

No presentation of Umbanda would be complete without a mention of the "fluids" surrounding a person and affecting his well-being. These fluids are energy and can be either positive or negative. The positive fluid entails qualities such as good, pleasant, healthy, beautiful, honest; the presence of the negative one is indicated by the appearance of suffering, of the qualities of bad, spoiled, frightening, or sick. All living beings, objects, deities, spirits, actions, and ideas can possess varying quantities of positive and negative fluids. Beings and also substances are capable of taking up fluids. Water, for instance, can be charged positively, and thus can have medicinal effects, or it may be contaminated because of having been used for ritual cleansing, and needs to be cautiously discarded. The positive charge of ritual objects must be renewed periodically. Cult sessions are saturated with positive fluids, and therefore represent a desirable environment for the spirits possessing the medium as well as for the visitors. The medium, of course, equally gains, because of being instrumental in creating the possibility for the spirit to be present. Mediums can draw negative fluids away from the patient by a movement of their hands, the famous "passes." Touching a statue on the altar lets the positive fluid flow into the person. Well-being results from a predominance of positive fluids, illness from the presence of negative fluids. Thus, the theory of fluids also helps in conceptualizing the cause and cure of disease, as, for instance, that the "evil eye" may pass bad fluids along to a person, thus causing trouble, or that an unhappy spirit might disturb the fluids in an individual. That will result not only in illness but also in personal problems. Such spirits need to be enlightened in an Umbanda center.

Illness can also come about in other ways, however. From Kardecism, Umbanda probably took the idea that illness may be the result of sins committed in a previous life. We mentioned the deleterious effect of black magic performed in Quimbanda. Being negligent in religious duties could be at the root of a problem. In that case the

respective spirit can be mollified by leaving a sacrificial offering of
food or drink at a particular place.

One of the best ways in which to become and remain well is to be
trained as a medium. Novices are trained by the cult leader and the
priests, that is, the fully trained mediums, during regular training
sessions. They are taught Umbanda theology, the categories of spirits,
what they are like and what they can do; the tasks of various group
leaders; how to prepare sacrificial offerings; and generally, the day-
by-day operation of the center.

Mediumistic training takes place first of all by demonstration, because of the novice's constant close association with possessed mediums at these training sessions. Much more clearly than during public
sessions, the novices hear the calls of the mediums to the spirits, their
murmured prayers, how they enter into trance and how they come
back, that is, how the spirit is sent away. There is a great deal of
singing, clapping, and drumming, which together with the culturally
produced expectation will induce the trance in many novices. Others
might need help from the cult leader, who will turn them around
until they become dizzy. After several weeks of this, head and chest
jerking is added, which is used both for initiating and terminating the
religious trance. The novices can gauge whether they are in trance by
perceiving changes in consciousness, slipping in and out, or possibly
becoming entirely amnesic, not remembering what they did or said.
For the client, the ideal is a fully amnesic medium, for that guarantees
complete confidentiality. Practiced mediums usually achieve a trance
of lesser intensity, where they are at least to some extent aware of what
the spirits say through their mouths.

In the course of training, various behavioral clues will now begin to
indicate which spirit has chosen a particular novice, and mediums
usually possessed by the respective being take over the schooling,
firming up the specific behavior associated with it. In other words, we
witness once more the sequence of establishing the trance first and
then creating and stabilizing the map. The manipulation of the novice
demonstrates that both the future medium and the spirit that will do
the possessing need to be trained. The novice might learn the typical
bent posture of the *prêto velho*, but the spirit is also enjoined not to be
rough with its future "horse." Inappropriate actions by a possessing
spirit are attributed to its insufficient training. As soon as the novice
indicates by behavior that full possession has taken place, other mediums will recognize that by handing the novice a cigar, sweet wine,
brandy, or whatever the respective spirit usually receives as a treat.

What the client sees in a public session is behavior specific to a
particular spirit, which makes it possible to identify it. *Caboclos*, Indians, that is, display protruded lips, a furrowed brow, eyes opening

and closing slowly; they might beat their chests or shoot imaginary arrows. A *criança* or child spirit skips, rolls, and tumbles. The *prêto velho* is feeble and stooped. The ordinary personality of the medium is temporarily obscured, and the changeover is total. As Figge tells:

> In various encounters, the deeply shocking differences in facial features were especially evident to me between the self-assured, superior, calm, happy spirits and their mediums, constrained to return to their oppressive and hopeless everyday life. In the spirit role, the majority of the mediums show a face that is fuller and smoother, the glance milder and more energetic. I may as well confess that on occasion I felt a truly tender, affectionate attachment to the *prêto velho*, as he was dishing out sometimes ordinary but always well-meaning advice to me like to a young relative. To my intense regret, this comforting feeling would then change into one of total estrangement and distancing, when the medium would return to ordinary consciousness and was once more the washerwoman, the single parent of three small children, or the resigned street vendor. Not only would they be more reserved toward me because the ranking order had been reversed, perhaps even expressing rejection, but as a matter of fact they looked entirely different, suddenly and effectively. (1973:155)

The type of scene that Figge alludes to would be played out at a public session. Such a session usually takes place in the evening and is a festive affair. As to physical setting, each center displays its name over the entrance, which usually contains the name of the saint, *orixá*, or spirit in charge of the premises. Outside the main entrance, there is a small altar dedicated to the *exu* spirits. Before entering the center, people greet the *exus* and place a small offering of food and drink to them into a box. Inside the brightly lit center, officials collect monthly dues of associates and have visitors sign the guest book.

The central room is divided by a wooden railing. Clients sit on wooden benches behind it in the back part, women on one side, men on the other. A few people carry flowers, cigars, or pipe tobacco to be presented to a spirit. The front part on the other side of the railing is reserved to the ritual activities of the spirits. There is an altar with statues of various *orixás*, saints, and spirits, together with flowers, candles, and a glass of water for absorbing bad fluids. Drums are ready next to the altar for calling the spirits.

After taking an ordinary bath in their homes, followed by a ritual one with seven herbs, the mediums assemble in the back of the center, where they change into their festive white clothes. They carry a towel for wiping the perspiration and wear strands of beads that represent the spirits of each medium. When all are ready, the cult leader opens the session. The drummers begin beating their drums, and the mediums start dancing to the rhythm. Songs to the various *orixás* and lesser spirits are intoned, with the audience joining in. An assistant brings in a silver censer on a chain and takes it to the altar, the drums, the mediums, and the audience to purify and to protect everyone against evil fluids that might have been carried into the center. Individually, the mediums prostrate themselves in front of the altar, are blessed by the cult leader, and kiss his hand. A collection is taken up, and after some more singing and drumming, the cult leader gives a brief sermon. Prayers are offered to Oxalá (Jesus) and some other spirit beings. Finally, an unaccompanied song, "to God and our Lady" opens the session, and with renewed drumming the spirits are called. Pressel describes the scene:

> Some mediums begin to spin around rapidly, and as their heads and chests jerk back and forth in opposing directions, the spirits lower themselves into their mediums. The hair of some female medium becomes disarrayed. Since it is the night of the Indian spirits, the facial expressions of what had been smiling mediums are transformed into the stern countenance of the caboclo spirits. Some of the Indians may move about as if they were shooting an imaginary arrow. They shout in the tongue of their "nation." The spirits may dance for a few minutes, greeting each other by touching each other's right and then left fore-arms. When the drumming stops, they find their places and wait for members of the audience to come for the consultation during which requests for help are made. The hands of the mediums rest behind their bodies, palms outward and fingers snapping impatiently. (1974:144)

Health and personal problems of every kind and description are brought to the consultations. The spirits prescribe herbs or other medicines and in some instances even perform "operations." At the end of the consultation, the client is cleansed of evil fluids by the spirit passing his right hand over the client's body. The session may last into the late hours of the night. Occasionally, a spirit possesses a member of the audience, causing the individual to shriek and shake. The cult leader will try to calm the spirit and may suggest the need for spiritual development and training as a medium.

Umbanda centers are also the scene of special feast days for various *orixás* throughout the year, for which those attending bring festive foods and liquor. Among the most popular is the one honoring the *orixá* Iemanjá, the goddess of the sea, but Christmas and Easter are equally celebrated.

The importance of Umbanda as a support network for its ad-herents cannot be overestimated. It offers, as we have seen, health care as well as social and psychological counseling. But Pressel finds that there is also a second level of significance. The various spirits represent the major ethnic heritages of Brazil, the *caboclos* the Brazilian Indians, the *prêtos velhos* the Africans, and the *exus* the immigrant strangers. Or, viewed differently,

> Some of my informants expressed the idea that the spirits were like the generations found in a family: "The indulgent prêto velho is like a grandfather; the stern caboclo is more like a father; and the child spirit is like a brother or sister." (1974:215)

In other words, the Brazilians who migrated to the cities in search of jobs, of opportunity, left behind something important, namely, the extended family. The spirits of Umbanda fill that painful social gap in their lives.

4 ENTECOSTALISM

A New Force in Christendom

Pentecostalism is another important possession religion in the modern world characterized by the experience of a positive possession by an otherworldly being or force. Compared to Umbanda or Spiritualism, the spread of the Pentecostal movement is overwhelming. Figures on Spiritualist membership nationally are not available, but a glance at the telephone book of a medium-size city such as Columbus, Ohio, my hometown, which has about 600,000 inhabitants, is certainly instructive: there are nine Spiritualist churches listed, as against fifty-two Pentecostal and sixty Apostolic congregations. And that is counting only the two principal Pentecostal denominations and not all the many smaller ones, such as Assemblies of God and others. John Thomas Nichol, an American historian, is obviously justified in calling Pentecostalism the third large force in Christendom, next to Catholicism and Protestantism.[1]

The start of the Pentecostal movement is usually attributed to Charles Fox Parham, although experiences similar to his appeared in the English-speaking world on both sides of the Atlantic at about the same time, and many events and personalities played a part. In this country, speaking in tongues is reported sporadically at least since the middle of the nineteenth century, later especially in the American Holiness movement, an outgrowth of revivals after the Civil War. Parham was born in Iowa in 1873. As a young man he was a lay preacher in the Congregational church. Later he joined the Methodists, and then the rapidly expanding Holiness movement. In 1900, he founded his Bethel Bible College in Topeka, Kansas. From scriptural studies he and his students became convinced that in Apostolic times a baptism by the Holy Spirit was always accompanied by the outward manifestation of speaking in tongues, and they wondered whether the same should not also be true in the modern age.

At the New Year's Eve service that year, an event occurred that convinced them that such was indeed the case. As Nichol describes it, one of Parham's students, Agnes Ozman, asked Parham to lay hands on her so that she might receive the Holy Spirit. He placed his hands on her head and prayed. Nichol quotes Parham:

> I had scarcely repeated three dozen sentences when a glory fell upon her, a halo seemed to surround her head and face, and she began speaking in the Chinese language, and was unable to speak English for three days.
>
> Seeing this marvellous manifestation of Pentecostal power, . . . we decided as a school to wait upon God. We felt that God was no respecter of persons and what He had so graciously poured out upon one, He would upon all. (1971:28)

We may surmise from this description that first of all, Parham entered the religious trance, inducing it in himself by intoning a prayer of at least "three dozen sentences." As a result, he began seeing a halo around the head and face of his student. Both by the prayer and by laying on of hands, and also because he was in trance himself, he then generated the trance in her, and in agreement with the cultural expectation that speaking in tongues would occur, she did produce glossolalia. But did she speak Chinese? It is not reported that any student in that Bible school in Topeka, Kansas, at the turn of the century spoke Mandarin, Pekingese, or any one of the many other Chinese languages current in that enormous country, and it is equally unlikely that the Reverend Parham did. Apparently no one thought it necessary to check. "Chinese" is often selected as the "unknown tongue," perhaps because it is exotic and from the other side of the world, and possibly also because of the shortness of the syllables of glossolalia, which conforms to a popular stereotype about what Chinese sounds like. A Spanish-speaking Apostolic minister in Yucatán, Mexico, also told me that he had used "Chinese" when he first spoke in tongues, and quoted his mother and their maid as witnesses; neither one had ever even met a Chinese speaker. Besides, if the member of a congregation speaking in tongues says it was Chinese, everyone assumes that he knows what he is talking about.

The characterization of glossolalia as a foreign language that could be understood if someone were present who spoke it is called *xenoglossia* and has biblical authority in the Acts of the Apostles, where the original story of Pentecost is told (Acts 2:4). It comes up so often in connection with the discussion of glossolalia, and plays such an important role not only in the thinking of Parham and his contemporaries but also in the belief system of present-day adherents of the Pentecostal movement, that we need to discuss it briefly at this point.

The xenoglossia hypothesis can be approached in a number of ways. One of these is linguistic. If the sequence of glossolalia syllables consists of, let us say, "la-la-la-la-la," then somebody might argue that it is French or Spanish, since in those languages *la* is the feminine article. However, just repeating an article does not constitute a message, and thus such an utterance cannot be called "French" or "Spanish." In other words, it is not a meaningful phrase of a natural language, it is merely vocalization. One might ask: What, then, is a natural language? Linguists agree on the following definition: A natural language combines speech sounds into minimal meaningful forms ("morphs," such as, for instance, words or endings) and strings these together into phrases by applying rules of grammar. Glossolalia utterances consisting of "la-la-la-la-la" do not conform to this description. That is true even when people produce sequences of syllables that are much more complex, as happens if they have spoken in tongues for years, and the excitation is minimal. Computer analysis of frequency of sounds and other traits always supports the contention that we are not dealing with utterances of a natural language.

Sometimes, however, people in trance will utter phrases that are meaningful but that are not part of their own mother tongue. How might that come about? The phenomenon in question has something to do with the nature of memory and recall. Human memory stores vast quantities of impressions. Psychologists maintain that we never actually forget anything that we ever perceived or experienced. However, usually only a small part of this memory content is at our disposal for retrieval. The religious trance, however, stimulates recall, making accessible long-buried material, in this case, of foreign speech.

What the Reverend Parham and his contemporaries found so fascinating about the "gift of tongues" was the idea that if God gave one utterance, he could go to China or to Russia, or to some other faraway heathen place, without knowing the respective language and yet be able to preach and be understood. As Parham is quoted as saying: "Anybody today ought to be able to preach in any language of the world if they had horse sense enough to let God use their tongue and throat"[2] (Nichol 1971:27). That was doubtless a very attractive prospect to English speakers, with their well-known aversion to language study. But the gift of tongues has never absolved missionaries from having to learn foreign languages. And it seems to me that the story of the Pentecost speaks of a miracle of an entirely different nature. When those Apostles left the building where they had been assembled and went outside to start preaching, it is reported that the multitude listening understood, although they spoke many different languages, Parthian, Median, Elamite, Phrygian, and even Latin. However, significantly, they shared a number of characteristics. They were all devout Jews who had come to be in Jerusalem for the holy days. The excitement of the important religious occasion prepared the ground for ecstasy; besides, it is to be assumed that they were accustomed to switching into trance, after all a common part of everybody's religious rituals at the time. The Apostles, still in intense trance themselves after their visions of fire descending on their heads and their speaking in tongues, induced it in the throng. The multitude, with the aid of the truly marvelous capabilities engendered in trance, then "understood" the core content of what they were preaching. Speaking in religious terms, the Holy Spirit using "the body," that is, the vocal apparatus of the Apostles, communicated to the listeners. A complex miracle of that sort would be difficult indeed to replicate.

Returning to Agnes Ozman's experience on that memorable New Year's Eve, we also learn that she could not speak English for three days after. In other words, the trance did not dissolve when she was finished speaking, or at the end of the ritual. That happens occasionally. The young man whose impressive motion pattern I filmed in an Apostolic temple in Mexico City (see chap. 1) had started speaking in tongues on a Friday evening, and did not return to Spanish until the following Tuesday when I filmed him. What I have often observed in people who are new to the ecstatic experience is that initially, their trance will be quite strong and tends to linger, although extreme cases such as the one in Mexico City and that of Agnes Ozman are relatively rare. Later, the energy level of the ecstasy becomes lower, and in many instances, the capacity disappears entirely within three to four years.

The importance of the experiences of Parham and his students, according to Nichol, lies in the fact that for the first time the concept of being baptized or filled with the Holy Spirit was linked to an outward sign, namely, that of speaking in tongues. The students and their preacher were so overwhelmed by it all, they dropped everything they were doing, everyone seeking to emulate Agnes Ozman's experience. Most of them succeeded. And since in the Scriptures, such events were said to signal the imminent end of the world and the Second Coming of Christ, the "Parhamites" embarked on a dedicated missionary effort trying to convert the world before it was too late. Although unsuccessful in the beginning, they began slowly to make headway, and in 1906 Parham was indirectly responsible for the renowned Azusa Street Revival.

This seminal event is linked to a student at Parham's new Bible school in Houston, Texas, namely, William J. Seymour, a Black Holiness preacher. When he became associate pastor of the Nazarene mission in Los Angeles, he started preaching on the baptism by the Holy Ghost and speaking in tongues, but ran into angry opposition from this Holiness congregation. They felt that they had already been baptized by the Holy Spirit and no new baptism was necessary. But after they locked him out of their church, he was invited by some dissenting members to preach in their homes instead. As Nichol tells it,

> There on April 9, 1906, seven seekers received the Holy Spirit baptism and commenced to speak in tongues. The records state that for three days and nights they shouted and praised God. People began to come from everywhere, forcing Seymour and his followers to procure an old frame building (once a Methodist church) on Azusa Street in the industrial section of Los Angeles. The building supplies that cluttered the hall were pushed aside; planks were placed upon empty nail kegs to provide seating space for the multitudes which came at ten o'clock in the morning (and often remained until three o'clock on the following morning), seeking salvation, sanctification, the Holy Spirit baptism, or healing. (1971:33)

The modest building at 312 Azusa Street became known the world over as the cradle of the Pentecostal movement. The Pentecostal experience, encompassing the baptism by the Holy Spirit, its outward manifestation in speaking in tongues, and associated "gifts of the Spirit," especially prophesy and healing, spread across the United States and to Canada. Recruits came not only from the Holiness movement but also from the mainline churches, the Episcopalians, Baptists, Methodists, Presbyterians, Lutherans, that is, from across the entire spectrum of Protestantism. Pentecostalism also provided new impetus to the various revivalistic movements in England. From there it spread to other European countries, especially to Norway, Finland, and Sweden, as well as to Germany and France. As early as 1914, it was brought to Tijuana by Mexicans converted in California. It spread all over Mexico, and soon, missionaries carried it also to Central and South America, especially to Chile and Brazil. The Pentecostal message found fertile ground in Africa, too, and took root even in such an unlikely place as Soviet Russia.

In the course of the ensuing decades, what at first seemed merely an attempt to revitalize existing denominations led to the founding of independent church organizations. These, in turn, split into many different sects, usually because of doctrinal disputes. In the years after the Second World War, Pentecostalism as a religious style experienced a strong resurgence and began spreading once more within the mainline churches, just as it had at its outset at the beginning of the century, this time even among Catholics. Some refer to this development as Neo-Pentecostalism; others speak of the Charismatic movement or the Charismatic Revival. Although Pentecostalism no longer occupies center stage in the popular press, it continues to play an extremely important role in the arena of modern religious life. The following description of an individual Latin-American Pentecostal (Apostolic) congregation and its history may bring this religious innovation into focus for us.

The Story of a Yucatecan Apostolic Congregation

Protestant missionizing on the Peninsula of Yucatán (Mexico) started shortly after the First World War, but the Pentecostal movement there is more recent. It is represented by a number of different branches in Yucatán, with the beginnings of the Apostolic denomination going back to 1959. After doing fieldwork and participant observation first with an Apostolic congregation in Indiana and then in Mexico City, I went to Yucatán in 1969, and there I have followed the fortunes of one particular Apostolic congregation (called below the "Temple Congregation") for sixteen years now, returning regularly every year.

The Temple Congregation is located in a small town, more rural than urban, of Maya Indians, in the northeast of Yucatán. The majority of the people are Catholic, but there is also a well-established Presbyterian congregation. Of the Pentecostal groups, the Apostolic one is the most prominent. By United States standards, the latter congregations are small, comprising no more than twenty-five to thirty adult members each.

The Apostolic membership is recruited from the stable lower middle class of this villagelike town. Proselytizing follows kinship lines, and almost everyone is related within a congregation. For instance, only four large extended families supply most of the adherents in the Temple Congregation. Reasons given for joining are personal preference; dislike of the Catholic church, which for some is still vaguely identified with the Spanish conquest; and "certainty," meaning that the experience of the actual presence "in one's body" of the Holy Spirit while speaking in tongues validates the belief system. Healing by prayer is a highly valued ritual often resorted to. Equally cherished by both men and women is personal participation in the activity in the temple, such as for the men the opportunity to lead a part of the service, and for both sexes especially the individual offering of a hymn "for the honor and glory of God," a privilege that can be denied to members as a measure of censure.

In 1969 the Temple Congregation was housed in a rectangular

mud-and-wattle house with a cement floor, built by the members. A few years ago, this structure was replaced by a cement-block building, also erected by the congregation. Inside, the temple is unadorned. The altar is a raised podium with a speaker's rostrum. In front of it but on the floor level, there is a small table with vases of flowers and two plates for the offering of money. Only the pastor may officiate on the podium. Men leading parts of the service stand behind this little table instead. For the worshipers, there are rows of wooden folding chairs, on the left for the women, on the right for the men. Women always wear scarves on their heads during the service.

Services take place every evening except on Friday, beginning sometime after sundown. The order of the worship service is fairly typical for this kind of congregation and agrees with that followed by others in Mexico and also in many Apostolic churches in the United States. Upon arrival, people go to kneel at the altar and say a prayer and then take their seats. When enough have assembled, one of the men assisting the pastor opens the service by calling for a hymn. That ends the animated conversations going on, but does not put a damper on the small children, who continue running and playing in the aisle and in the space at the back of the church, until they finally come to sleep at their mothers' feet on the cool cement floor. Under the direction of the same or another assistant, there are an offering of testimonies, the reading of a text from the Bible with the assistant and the congregation alternating, the presenting of personal hymns, a communal prayer with all praying in their own words, more hymns, taking the offering to the table, and then the "altar call," a lengthy prayer with all adults going to kneel at the podium. This is the ritually marked occasion for speaking in tongues: it will not be done at any other time during the service. Vocalization may become quite loud, but except for an occasional raising of arms, movement is quite restrained. Not everyone speaks in tongues; some listen even while they pray and comment afterwards on how beautiful it was, or "how grandly the Holy Spirit has manifested itself today." The altar call comes to an end with the pastor ringing a small bell. Praying in tongues stops, and the worshipers return to their seats. After another hymn, the pastor preaches a lengthy sermon. A final hymn concludes the service, which usually lasts at least two hours or more. If there is sickness, the pastor may now call those wishing to be healed to come forward, and he and a number of the parishioners will pray for them.

People learn speaking in tongues principally during special prayer sessions for the Holy Spirit. Pastors making a special effort at teaching it are rare. Usually, it is learned by imitation, facilitated by strong motivation—without the baptism of the Holy Spirit, one cannot enter into heaven—and by the acoustic driving provided by the strongly rhythmic singing, clapping, and extremely loud guitar music.[3] The combination of these factors induces the trance, and in an additional step, the vocalization is then superimposed. No personality traits are imputed to the Holy Spirit, except that it is easily offended and then will no longer descend into the worshiper. Most of the time there is no indication what the offense against the Holy Spirit might have been, and there are no stories told about any specific personal communications. Testimonies speak in general terms about blessings received, or about having been healed. Much is made of "conversion" in this context in the literature, and one might think of conversion as a flipping or changing of the particular map. However, if a new brain map is formed at all, it must be quite ephemeral. Knowing the members of this congregation quite well and over such a long time suggests to me that at least in this case, "conversion" does not mean turning an old Adam/Eve into a new one. At most, there is a change of certain habits, such as giving up drinking any alcoholic beverages or going to picture shows.

The Temple Congregation was founded in 1960. In the course of its history, it went through a number of changes. Recruitment of members was very slow in the beginning and did not pick up until 1969, with the arrival of an energetic young preacher. *Hermano* ("Brother") Lorenzo (not his real name) was an efficient teacher of speaking in tongues and an impassioned orator, whose sermons concerned mainly the baptism of the Holy Spirit and the Second Coming. Under his direction, the congregation soon increased its membership to more than eighty, with both men and women speaking in tongues. By early 1970, however, conflicts developed between Lorenzo and the congregation over money matters, always a sore point in these extremely cash-poor congregations. The congregation felt rejected by its charismatic leader, and the resulting crisis brought on a mass trance event, with several of the leading men having visions and predicting the end of the world in September of 1970.[4] The events had repercussions beyond the local level, and eventually four other congregations also joined in the trance upheaval. The mass trance dissolved about forty days later, at about the projected date for the end of the world. When the prophesy failed, many newly recruited members left the congregation, which shrank to its precrisis level. Lorenzo joined another sect, which predicted the Second Coming for a later date. Some of the leading men of the upheaval formed groups of their own. Others lost interest in religious activity altogether and "returned to the world." None became Catholic again.

For a while after these trying events, the members of the Temple

Congregation were afraid to speak in tongues in their own church. They blamed Satan for what had happened during the upheaval and felt that when they spoke in tongues during the crisis, Satan had insinuated himself. It had not been the Holy Spirit at all who had given directions at that time. Instead they spoke in tongues during private prayer services at home, or when visiting other congregations.

There were also problems higher up in the organization. The ministers had the obligation to send half of all offerings to the district headquarters of the Apostolic Church in Villahermosa. There the drop in membership following the crisis showed up as a decrease in revenues. To remedy the situation, it was decided to transfer the seventeen Yucatecan ministers, who were thought to be "soft" on their congregations in money matters, out of Yucatán and to replace them with ministers from Tabasco. In view of the cultural gulf separating Yucatán from the neighboring state of Tabasco, the result was predictable: Infuriated, the Yucatecans under the leadership of Luis Lugo, one of the founders of the Apostolic church in Yucatán, in 1974, seceded from the Iglesia Apostólica del Fe en Cristo Jesus, the Apostolic church, and founded their own organization. The obligation for sending offerings was abolished, and Luis Lugo and his brother, both men of relative affluence, started to support indigent preachers out of their own pockets to ease the burden on the local congregations. This system continues to this day.

At the central administration of the Apostolic church in Mexico City, the secession was apparently blamed on undesirable doctrinal independence produced by the ecstatic behavior. To put a stop to further defections, Bishop Gajiola sent out a pastoral letter to all congregations directing them to deemphasize speaking in tongues. After all, the Holy Spirit had manifested itself sufficiently; there was no need for any more manifestations. "They must have a very tired dove," the minister of the Temple Congregation quipped.

Actually, their own dove was not all that vigorous either any more. But a strong revival occurred in 1977, when a dance movement spread to all the Apostolic congregations of Yucatán. Its source was not clear: According to some, it originated in the north of Mexico; others said it came from Honduras. Emulating King David's dance before the Ark of the Covenant, the rapidly swelling Yucatecan congregations danced a shuffling two-step, rocking back and forth to a series of lovely, rhythmical short hymns, called *coritos*, and soon were transported into trance and speaking in tongues.

The dance episode was short-lived, however, lasting only about three years. Since 1980, there has been no more dancing, and the number of people speaking in tongues at the Temple Congregation has steadily decreased, as did the membership. The decline has been hastened by the new minister, Hermano Manuel (not his real name), who is adamantly opposed to speaking in tongues. He silenced the last two women, members since 1970, who were still speaking in tongues, by telling them that they were motivated only by vanity. He has not preached a single sermon about the baptism of the Holy Spirit or about speaking in tongues. He and his coterie have abolished birthdays and weddings in the church, and there is no Easter celebration or Christmas, because "none of this is biblical." He is turning the congregation away from Pentecostalism and toward an extreme brand of fundamentalism, and the same trend has also been noted at a few other Yucatecan congregations. At the Temple Congregation there is rancor, too, because although all preachers are by tradition supposed to work for a living, Manuel wants to feed his large family on the offerings and tithing alone, castigating those who do not contribute enough. "What kind of a church is this?" an old-timer complained. "All the preacher does is scold and exhort, there is no love any more, and no joy."

The story of the Yucatecan Temple Congregation demonstrates some important aspects of this modern Christian possession religion. Simple answers to the question of why people are attracted to it, such as those offered by behavioral scientists when analyzing Spiritualism or Umbanda—the uprooting of rural populations, industrialization, loss of family ties, painful culture change, search for a health-care system, and upward mobility or economic advantages—may fit in the large cities. But Pentecostalism also spreads where none of these conditions prevail. The Temple Congregation is by no means a case of one. The World Council of Churches offers the following interpretation:

> The emergence and growth of Independent Churches in Africa, of Pentecostal Churches and of Pentecostalism within the established Churches could point to some deficiency of traditional Roman Catholicism and Protestantism. Theology and practice of these Churches has to a large extent neglected the Holy Spirit, except for some standard affirmation about his continuing presence. . . . The doctrine of the Holy Spirit and even more the sensitivity to his active presence in the Church and the world were and still are underdeveloped in the western tradition of Christianity.[5]

If we substitute *ecstatic experience* for *Holy Spirit* in the above statement, we begin to see that beyond the disastrous cultural changes that we are subject to in this century, the Pentecostal movement highlights a conflict that was inherent in the Christian church from its inception.

We can take it all the way back to that incident related by the Apostle John, where after his resurrection, Jesus appears to the disciples, and Thomas, who had not been present, will not believe it:

> A week later the disciples were once more in the room, and this time Thomas was with them. Despite the locked doors, Jesus came and stood before them. "Peace be with you," he said; then, to Thomas: "Take your finger and examine my hands. Put your hand into my side. Do not persist in your unbelief, but believe!" Thomas said in response, "My Lord and my God!" Jesus then said to him:
>> "You became a believer because
>> you saw me.
>> Blest are they who have not seen
>> and have believed." (20:29)

The core of the conflict is that of the need for experience as against believing without seeing. We might say that Pentecostalism is the latest attempt in Christianity to try and remedy what could be called "ecstasy deprivation," rebelling against a divine service that does not include the trance. Throughout Christian history, there have been individual revolts against this deprivation, in the form of mysticism, or the visions of the saints, for instance. In situations of a generalized crisis, ecstatic experiences of individuals lead to the founding of new sects, a frequent occurrence, e.g., during the Reformation.

Curiously, however, as we saw also in the Yucatecan example, sects that start out with the institutionalization of the ecstatic experience eventually give up their hard-won innovation and return to "orthodoxy and discipline." For a centralized organization, this turn of events is highly desirable, and the history of Christianity shows that all means, fair and foul, have been used to purge the Church of ecstatics. That such attempts have been uniformly successful, and that renouncing ecstasy happens regularly even without intervention from above,[6] could be the result of a hitherto unrecognized factor. It may be related directly to the nature of the Holy Spirit as a possessing entity of the alternate reality. The Holy Spirit is not a spirit of the dead; it is not a grandfatherly spirit listening to personal problems, or a colorful *exu* or *orixá*. It is power only, a mighty wind. It "fills" and "moves" people. There is trance, and there is the ability to vocalize. But probably, as I mentioned above, there is no brain map, or there is only a very weak one, created while people learn to speak in tongues. And so all the Apostolic groups that I have come to know have a body of lore about people losing the ability for ecstasy. In this the Pentecostals differ greatly from non-Christian religious communities, where once triggered, the experience of ecstasy remains accessible throughout life. If Pentecostalism should fade from the scene, we can expect some other ecstatic movement to take its place, because quite clearly, the need for religious experience is deeply and indeliby embedded in our humanness. And over and over again, it will become extinguished.

5 THE DANGEROUS SPIRITS OF JAPAN

From the benevolent spirits experienced in possession by Spiritualists, Umbandists, and Pentecostals, we now pass on to another class of spirit beings, namely, the dangerous ones. Powerful, but neither absolutely good nor absolutely evil, they represent humanity's horticulturalist heritage (see chap. 2). They can and most of the time do act in a friendly manner, and thus on the face of it there seems to be little to distinguish them from the kindly entities we have come to know. But if crossed, they may become threatening, and it is this potential for mischief, this perceived underlying threat, that marks them as qualitatively different. They may even start out causing harm, but then turn around and come to be helpful friends. To us Westerners, whose thinking is schooled by a pervasive good/bad categorization, it is sometimes disconcerting how in a particular story a spirit who to our way of perceiving the world is clearly up to no good can still be classed as benevolent. The ancient *exu* spirits of Umbanda retain some of this peculiar scintillation, but they are mainly known to anthropologists from their study of surviving small horticulturalist societies, for instance in South America. Of the large modern industrial societies, Japan is the only one where they still play an important role, appearing in many of the modern sects called in the literature the *New Religions*.

Japan's native faith is called Shinto, which is a Chinese loan word. The second part of the word *Shinto, to,* means "way." In Japanese classification this term distinguishes Shinto from "religion," in that it has neither a known founder nor a "book," or a body of dogma, and it emphasizes the qualitative difference between the body of folk traditions, the life way represented by Shinto, and a formal religious system such as Buddhism. As to the *shin* part of the Chinese term, the Japanese give *kami* as a translation. Some Western writers insist on translating *kami* by "god." This is accurate when referring to the Sun Goddess, for instance, or to some other deity of that nature, but that is only one of its meanings. It may also stand for "ghost," a spirit of the dead, such as might reside in a local shrine, perhaps of a long-departed samurai, or of particularistic spirits surviving from the horticulturalist past, who created a certain region, island, or mountain, and who also have their own shrines. Or it can indicate the quality of the sacred, of the world of spirits, or that which touches the other dimension. Thus, it might describe a person in contact with spirits, as in the case of a religious leader, Kitamura Sayo, who was called Ōgamisama, with *Ō* indicating respect; the middle term *gami (kami)* pointing to the sacred connection, or to the conviction that she is a *kami;* and *sama* an honorific form of *san*, added as a marker to the name of a person, as we do with Mr. or Mrs. So instead of translating *Shinto* as "the way of the gods," it would be less confusing to speak of "the way of the spirits," or just to leave it as "the way of the *kami*."

In the seventh and eighth centuries, Buddhism was superimposed on this diffuse traditional way of the spirits. Much is made in Western writings of the syncretism between the two religions, and although it is extensive, the meld is incomplete even today, as any visitor to Japan can easily tell.[1] A large Buddhist sacred precinct may contain a strikingly different small Shinto shrine, for instance. The point is important, because as we shall see, some New Religions are obviously derived from Buddhism, while others have equally undisguised Shinto origins.

Western writers talking about the numerous New Religions that began appearing in Japan after the middle of the last century like to call attention to the fact that in Japanese history, new sects have tended to arise with every major social or political and economic crisis. But that is not peculiar to Japan. Quite generally, religious innovation tends to arise everywhere in times of stress. In other words, it is not the culture of the respective society, or even the particulars of the problem, but rather that people perceive themselves in a dead-end, utterly desperate situation that generates this type of religious response. The "enthusiastic" sects of nineteenth-century America we mentioned in connection with the history of Spiritualism (see chap. 2) are a case in point. New religions appeared with equal regularity also in Europe. There, however, popular reaction in the form of a new sect or movement was often aborted because of the determined opposition of the powerful Catholic church to sectarianism, so that uncounted would-be religious innovators, the early Czech reformer

John Huss, for instance, the pantheistic Italian philosopher and monk Giordano Bruno, or the German Anabaptist Thomas Münzer, to name just a few, ended up at the stake or on the gallows instead.

Although in Japan, religious innovation was also often suppressed, neither the Shinto temples nor Buddhism had quite the same power as the Inquisition. Crisis reactions in the form of new sects appear there in the historical record as early as A.D. 794. That was a time of great social unrest that eventually led to moving the capital of the country from Nara to Kyoto. Large numbers of unconventional sects arose also at the time of internal upheaval in connection with the rebellion of the Fujiwara, when the capital was moved again, this time from Kyoto to Kamakura around A.D. 1200, and during the time of the civil war in 1550–1600, when historical sources for the first time give clear indication that possession cults were also part of the picture. The historian Anesaki, a Buddhist priest, speaks with abhorrence of "magic, sorcery, *exorcism*, and divination" when describing the new sects of that era. Obviously, one needs no exorcism unless there is prior possession.

Another powerful wave of New Religions began about 1870, after the Meiji restoration and the severe traumatization of Japanese society as the country opened its gates to the West; it received a boost from the events in the middle 1920s, when Japan suffered catastrophic economic problems; and it rose to new heights after the Second World War, which ended in the first military defeat in Japanese history. In the decade after the end of American occupation, as many as 360 New Religions were registered. At least 150 were recognized in 1966 by the Japanese Ministry of Education, and according to the *Religion Yearbook*, the combined membership of these cults or sects amounted to about twenty-nine million people at that time. In 1970, the American sociologist James W. White[2] put the figure of incorporated religious organizations at over one thousand, claiming more than fifteen million believers. Some of these statistics are probably inflated by enthusiastic adherents. Discrepancies arise also because while there are organizations that list individual members, others count households. Besides, as some authors point out, it is entirely acceptable in Japan to belong to a number of different groups simultaneously, while it is taken for granted that the family would continue participating in Buddhist rituals and retain its relationship with a particular Shinto temple. All this introduces additional inaccuracies. But no matter how the actual figures add up, it is obvious that we are dealing with a process of significant proportions in modern Japanese life.

The largest movement usually listed among the New Religions is Sōka Gakkai. It is also the best-known in the West, because it carries out extensive missionary activity outside of Japan. However, it is quite untypical of the New Religions, which are openly syncretic, being intolerant and nationalistic in the extreme. It is in fact a Buddhist revival and bears the marks of the Nichiren sect of Buddhism of the thirteenth century, from which it arose. Important for our context, it has no institutionalized possession. We will demarcate the category of the New Religions somewhat more narrowly, excluding Sōka Gakkai and other similar sects and concerning ourselves only with those that exhibit possession.

The forces creating the typical New Religions are quite different from those fueling the growth of Sōka Gakkai. New Religions are tolerant, eclectic, and, as White puts it, "vague as regards the border between the natural and the supernatural" (1970:21). White summarizes the salient factors:

> The new religions as a collective phenomenon indicate that religious sentiment as many Japanese perceive it cannot be expressed or fulfilled through the orthodox religious channels. . . . In Japan the traditional faiths are . . . the repositories of traditions, of abstruse philosophy and sterile theology far removed from the daily life of the common people. Shinto, as a unifying spiritual system, has not recovered from the blow dealt it by military defeat and subsequent discredit. The established Buddhist sects have never regained the vitality they demonstrated in the fourteenth century. And Christianity, which had had a genuine impact when it was introduced in the sixteenth century, became, after its readmittance in the Meiji era, no more than an imported theological system dispensed by foreigners—attractive to intellectuals but unappealing to the masses. In fact, if one seeks living religion in contemporary Japan, there are very few places to look for it outside of the new religions. (1970:20–21)

The New Religions have a number of traits in common.[3] They proclaim the goal of establishing a perfect world here and now and promise material prosperity to those who join. They are easy to enter; their teachings are simple and not difficult to follow. They work in small groups as well as impressive mass assemblies. Their organization is highly centralized and focuses on a single leader. It is this leader who gives each movement its distinctive character. They have large, elaborate centers, which serve as places of pilgrimage and make effective use of mass media of communication. Their membership is recruited from the lower middle class, especially middle-aged and older women, although a number of them also list upper-middle-class adherents and find interested followers among young people. Their rituals have a festive air about them and facilitate the entrance into the religious trance.

Most important, however, the New Religions promise the preven-

tion and healing of disease. It is estimated that between sixty and
seventy percent of those participating in the New Religions join initially because of illness, many of them stress-related and psychosomatic in nature. Illness is usually believed to be caused by possession
by evil spirits, unhappy ghosts, or spirits of animals. Especially the
latter trait is again derived from the horticulturalist heritage in Japanese culture, where humans and animals are not separated by the
same insuperable wall as in the later agriculturalist traditions. One of
the possessing animal spirits, for instance, is the fox.[4] It is a prime
example of a dangerous spirit entity. On the one hand, possession by
it is believed to cause frightening feelings of suffocation and inexplic-
able waves of body heat. On the other hand, the fox is the messenger
of Inari, the God of Wealth (formerly of rice); I saw a shrine to it next
to a computer in a spacious hall on the outskirts of the city of
Kurashiki, where farmers auction off their produce every morning.
Other animal spirits involved in possession are toads, snakes, or
badgers, even house cats. While possession causes illness, followers
may also consult with the possessing spirits and receive advice on
pressing personal and work-related problems. Thus, these religious
movements are tailored precisely to the needs of people caught in
rapid culture change.

Almost without exception, the new sects start out with their
founder, usually but not always a woman, undergoing a religious, an
ecstatic, experience. Even in childhood, these individuals exhibit
marks of their future calling. They are sickly, odd, weak, until they
have a climactic mystic experience. Quoting the British social anthropologist Carmen Blacker, who did extensive participant observation and literature studies on Japanese shamanistic practices in the
1960s,

> A deity, by means of a dream or a possession, seizes them and claims
> them for his service. Thenceforward they are changed characters.
> Their former oddity and sickliness give way to a remarkable strength
> and magnetism of personality, which is conferred on them, together
> with various supernormal powers, by the deity who has possessed them
> and who henceforth governs their lightest move. The exercise of these
> powers and the proclamation of the deity's message result in the course
> of time in believers gathering round and forming a new sect.
> (1975:129)

Blacker recounts the biographies of several women who became
founders of new cults or religions. One of the earliest and most
famous is Nakayama Miki (her first name, Miki, is given last in
Japanese usage), the founder of Tenrikyō, now the largest and richest
of the New Religions originating in the early nineteenth century. She

was born in 1798. A shy and introspective girl, she was married at thirteen to a man she disliked, and whose mother tyrannized her. Two of her daughters died, and then, in 1837, her only son fell seriously ill with severe pain in his legs. When conventional medical treatment failed, she called in a mountain ascetic and healer to perform an exorcism. This ritual involved the recitation of sutras and mantras, which would force the malicious spirit causing the illness to leave the patient and to enter a medium. The spirit could then be interrogated as to its identity and reasons for causing the affliction. One night in September of 1838, however, the medium could not come, and Miki, who had worked as a healer herself, offered to take her place.

> As the spells began to get under way Miki's face suddenly changed and she fell into a violent state of trance. To the question as to what deity was possessing her she answered, "I am Ten-no-Shogun."
> "What manner of god might Ten-no-Shogun be?" they asked.
> "The original true god who has descended from heaven to save all mankind," the deity answered through Miki's mouth. It then demanded that Miki's body should be given over as a shrine for its own use. Miki's husband, much taken aback, replied that such a request was impossible to grant, since Miki was the mother of four children, the youngest only a few months old. The god thereupon threatened that if its orders were disobeyed it would blast the whole family with curses.
> For three days after this exchange Miki is said to have been in an uninterrupted state of possession, sitting bolt upright transmitting the god's answers to questions without touching a drop of water or a grain of rice. Eventually her husband saw no alternative but to capitulate, and formally renounce to the god his responsibility for his wife. At once Miki returned to her normal state of consciousness. (1975:131)

After this initial possession, Miki continued having similar experiences. She also started giving away everything the family owned, apparently upon divine command, even having the family home torn down. If her demands were refused, she reacted with severe convulsions. These actions constituted her initiation. Some years after its completion, it was discovered that she possessed miraculous healing powers, especially granting painless childbirth. Her fame spread, and with the help of an adherent, Izo Iburi, an efficient administrator, her following was organized into a fast-growing sect. In 1869 she started writing a very long poem in trance, an *Ofudesaki* or transmission of her revelations. It took fifteen years to complete, and together with other revelations it formed the body of teachings of her sect, which was officially recognized a few years after her death in 1887.

As a second example, let us look at the life of Kitamura Sayo, called Ōgamisama, the founder of Tensho Kōtai Jingukyō, popularly known as the Dancing Religion. She was born to a farmer's family in 1900 and

at twenty was married to a weak and colorless man, whose mother
mistreated and starved her outrageously.

> [She started] various ascetic religious practices, which she continued
> for a couple of years until in 1944 she became aware that there was
> another being inside her body with conversed with her and ordered
> her about. This entity announced itself to be a snake by the name of
> Tobyo. It explained many things to her, of the past and the future and
> of her previous lives. It also gave correct weather forecasts and lessons
> in laundering and cooking, together with useful advice on diet and
> vitamins. Its advice was always good, but if for any reason Ōgamisama
> were to disobey its commands she was immediately racked with agonis-
> ing pains. [Thomsen quotes her as telling that it would say, "If you
> disobey me, I will kick your stomach to give you internal hemorrhage,
> or I shall beat your head and give you cerebral hemorrhage. Which do
> you prefer?" (1963:201)] She soon found that she only had to open her
> mouth for sermons and songs to pour forth from the being inside her.
> (1975:135)

The early life of the founder of the powerful Ōmoto sect, Deguchi
Nao, born in 1837, is also characterized by frightful suffering in
childhood, poverty, a disastrous marriage, and the deaths of several of
her eleven children. In 1890 one of her married daughters went
insane, and the following year the same fate befell her eldest daughter.

> A few days after this latest and culminating disaster, in January 1892,
> Nao had a vivid dream that she was wandering in the spirit world. A
> day or two later she fell suddenly into a violent state of trance. Her
> body almost tore apart with the strain, she leapt up and down from a
> sitting position while loud roars like those of a wild beast burst from
> the pit of her stomach. In the course of this seizure an extraordinary
> dialogue is said to have taken place between her own voice and the
> terrible "stomach" voice of the deity inside her. The god announced its
> name to be Ushitora-no-Konjin, and to have come into Nao's body in
> order that the present hideous state of the world should be trans-
> formed into a paradise. (1975:133)

After this initial possession, she continued with similar episodes,
roaming wildly through her village. Finally, she was confined to a
room in her house for forty days. She quieted down and began
scratching texts into the pillars. She continued writing during the next
twenty-seven years of her life, and her revelations grew into an im-
mensely long *Ofudesaki*, the sacred text of her sect. After her release
from confinement, she was discovered to have miraculous healing
powers. Her following quickly grew, forming the nucleus for what

later became Ōmotokyō. After she was joined by another gifted organizer, Ueda Kisaburo, who married one of her daughters, changing his name to Deguchi Onisaburō, Ōmotokyō gained national importance, becoming one of the most influential of the New Religions, from which a number of other cults eventually split off.

When we consider the powerful possession experiences of these founders, it seems odd that descriptions of the movements they founded contain so little reference to possession behavior and exorcism. Quite possibly, the fault lies with authors of the reports about them, principally because of lack of adequate fieldwork. Harry Thomsen, for instance, whose compendium is often quoted, was a missionary with the Christian Mission to Buddhists. For his work, he studied the English and Japanese literature on the subject. In addition, he tells, he spent "a few days at the headquarters of each religion in order to penetrate into the peculiar atmosphere of each one." He added some visits to outlying churches or temples. Understandably, by collecting data in such a haphazard fashion, he leaves us with nothing more than the skeleton of the organization and physical setup together with some tantalizing but inadequate impressions.

Tenrikyō (the -kyō ending means "religious teaching"), the religion founded by Nakayama Niki, is a case in point. In 1960, it claimed a membership of more than two million. The daily services at the sanctuary in Tenry City follow Shinto lines. They start out with an offering of vegetables, fruit, fish, rice cakes, and sake (rice wine). There is a solemn procession led by the spiritual head of the religion, followed by a prayer recited by him. This is followed by the high point of the service, a masked dance carried out by ten performers in a recessed section reenacting the creation of the world. Are the masked dancers possessed during this dance? They might well be, but we are not told. A sermon extols the life and thoughts of the founder. Stretching the point a bit, "possession" is represented by dust, which humans keep piling on the world by carrying on wars, and on their souls with their selfishness, competitiveness, and suffering. In an exorcistic ritual repeated in every Tenrikyō service, whether public or private, is a prayer for the blessing of the Parent God, accompanied by a special hand movement, which brushes away this dust.

In Tensho Kōtai Jingukyō, the "Dancing Religion," the possession complex is harder to overlook. Its membership is predominantly rural and in 1960 was put at about 110,000. It is highly syncretic in its teachings, combining Shinto and Buddhist elements. Its headquarters are at the founder's farmhouse in the village of Tabuse in the south of Japan. The services feature the Ōgamisama's sermons, prayers, and the dance. She preaches without any preparation, often entirely in poetry, giving voice to her possessing deity, Tensho Kōtai Jingo. This deity was originally a Shinto god of rather limited power, who was generalized by her as the "Absolute God of the Universe."

Humans are believed to be possessed by harmful spirits, representing the "six roots of evil," which are expelled during a prayer composed by Ōgamisama. Trance is instituted during this prayer: "The believers work themselves into complete religious ecstasy, tears run down their cheeks, and their limbs vibrate. They shake their hands and lift them above their heads over and over again in vehement movements" (Thomsen 1963:208). As to the origin of this prayer behavior, Thomsen quotes a publication of the organization, the *Prophet of Tabuse:*

> In the beginning Ōgamisama prayed [the above prayer] to expel evil spirits, but later on, all the comrades joined her in prayer. During the course of such earnest prayer a most wonderful phenomenon occurred among the comrades. Their clasped hands quivered up and down involuntarily as they prayed. At first they were surprised at these unaccountable movements, but Ōgamisama explained that "it is a psychic activity. When your hands are shaking high at your breast it means that your living spirit is activated. When the unconverted or stray spirits of the dead influence you, your hands will shift downward and will make downward movements. But as soon as these spirits are converted or leave you for a moment, your hands will rise above your head." (1963:208)

The trance dance that made this religion famous, however, is not a possession ritual. It is called the "Dance of Non-ego" and is intended instead "to take the adherent inside the gate of the Kingdom of God." It is believed to redeem the performers as well as all the evil spirits of the world.

Deguchi Nao's Ōmotokyō had a tragic history. At one time it was nearly wiped out by government repression; its buildings were razed and its leaders jailed as retribution for the antiwar stance of Deguchi Kisaburō (also called Onisaburō), Nao's son-in-law and master organizer of the movement. He is well known in Japan also outside of Ōmoto as a result of a lengthy and graphic account of his extensive spirit journey.[5] Ōmoto reached its greatest expansion between the two world wars, when it had in excess of two million members. It is much smaller now, but still quite important, especially because it has provided the inspiration for a number of daughter movements. Ōmotokyō combines elements from both Buddhism and Shinto, but the principal message of the entire Ōmoto group is based on the founder's revelation that the final destruction of the world is at hand, and that after the fall and a thorough cleansing, a better world would be constructed through the good offices of the leader of the movement acting as the savior.

After the Second World War, two Ōmoto centers were built at Kameoka and Ayabe, near Kyoto. The large communal services at these centers are Shinto in character, but on the local level the principal ritual activity of Ōmoto has from the start been healing by means of exorcism. In outline, such a service consists of the minister of the church bowing before a Shinto altar; he claps his hands, intones a prayer. There is a "salvation song," then one relating the creation of the world. After that, the minister asks the supplicant his name, address, age, and nature of affliction. Next he turns toward the altar and reports this information to the deity. He then takes a rice ladle wrapped in red paper and and moves it slowly around the body of the patient to cleanse it.

In view of the dearth of information on the New Religions based on fieldwork and participant observation, it is of special importance that Winston Davis, an American sociologist, published his research results gathered with a descendent group of Ōmoto.[6] The religion is called Sukyō Mahikari, or "True-Light Supra-Religious Organization." He studied it in a six-month period in 1976, in a provincial town he calls Nakayama (not its real name). The group is represented in many cities of Japan. It also has missionary outposts in Europe, the Americas, and North Africa, mainly working with Japanese immigrants. In 1970, it claimed a membership of about 400,000.

The founder of Sukyō Mahikari, Okada Yoshikazu, later called Kotama, was born to a Samurai family in 1901. He graduated from a military academy and served in the Pacific War. During the campaign in Indochina, he fell from his horse and injured his back. He was diagnosed as having tuberculosis of the spine and was given only three years to live. He was cured by an amulet from one of the New Religions, however, which was said to transmit "spirit rays." In 1959 he unexpectedly developed a high fever and became unconscious:

> Suddenly he found himself transported to the astral world, where he saw an old man with white hair standing in a white cloud and washing clothes in a golden tub. Later, Okada interpreted this vision as a revelation of Su-god ("the Lord God") and of the cleansing mission that was about to be entrusted to him. Five days after the vision, on his birthday, Okada was awakened at five o'clock in the morning by a divine voice saying, "Get up. Change your name to Kotama (Jewel of Light). Raise your hand. Trials and tribulations are coming." (1980:5)

Okada thought of this vision as a revelation instructing him to heal by raising his hand and thereby expelling evil, illness-causing spirits.

He began his healing activity, while at the same time, always at night, his ecstatic experiences continued. He jotted everything down, writing in trance at an enormous speed. These writings were later collected and constitute the sacred script of the movement today. He started recruiting converts, and within ten years, Sukyō Mahikari became a nationwide movement. It gained additional momentum when in 1968 he demonstrated his purification method on an afternoon television program. He died in 1974, appointing his daughter as his successor shortly before his death.

Mahikari is a predominantly urban movement, recruiting its members from the lower middle class, especially from among middle-aged and older women. However, according to Davis's figures, men are more consistent than women in attending the meetings, they take more higher-level courses, and the highest positions of authority and responsibility in the local groups are dominated by them (1980:244). As in all New Religions, the dropout rate is high—in the Nakayama group as much as fifty percent; another thirty percent are only lukewarm—so that the head of a local center can count on no more than about twenty percent as a steady membership (1980:229). The principal reason for joining is sickness, with fifty-two percent; the interest in "miracles," that is, miraculous healing, in coincidences and windfalls, in spirits, and in religion runs behind with twenty-two, eighteen, and eleven percent respectively.

The principal shrine of Mahikari is in Tokyo. Local centers organize mass meetings, too, but most of the work is done in relatively small groups. Davis describes the first demonstration meeting at the local center that became the object of his study. Members of the group greeted him and other new arrivals at the street corner. They were guided to a modest public hall. As is customary in Japan, they took off their shoes and entered the carpeted room. On the television screen a healing session was going on, with a woman treating a man sitting opposite her, his hands together as if in prayer. As the woman raised her palms toward him, he began going into trance, swaying, writhing, shaking his head violently. Similar scenes were also being enacted in the hall, where snatches of conversation overheard indicated that people were talking about various illnesses and misfortune.

> Two friendly young women materialized and offered to demonstrate what the Treatment was all about. We were asked to place our hands and feet together, the left thumb covering the right, the big toe of our left foot over the big toe of our right. . . . We closed our eyes, and the young ladies, now sitting opposite us, clapped their hands three times and began to recite what sounded like a Shinto incantation. After this, nothing seemed to happen. I presumed that they were holding their hands over us. . . .

[A few minutes later] the young woman in front of me quietly began to sing a slow and soothing song that sounded like a melancholy folksong. At first I thought that she was singing to me. But no. I suddenly realized that she was addressing "spirits" inside me:

Comrade spirits! Cast off all earthly attachments;
Perform your ascetic discipline [*shugyō*] in the spirit world.
If you leave sin and impurities behind you in the world
In the astral world you will suffer all the more.
  Painful as it is, every time you rid yourself of attachment
You get one step closer to paradise.
If, because of your attachment to this world, you possess someone's body,
You will be punished for the sin of escaping from the astral world.
There is no road to hell as terrible as that of attachment;
Behold the dawning of the spirit world and serve God!
If you do not get rid of your attachment to this world,
Repeated cycles of death and rebirth will be your fate until you fall into hell.
For the happiness of the lovely wife and child you left behind,
Devote yourself to fulfilling your obligations in the other world.
Within the hearts of your surviving family,
Create the desire to serve God's Mahikari faith.
Know that God has a prayer for saving
Hopeless lives and incurable diseases.

After the song was over, my partner was quiet for a few minutes. Then, in a loud, authoritative voice she pronounced the word *oshizumari* (Peace, be still!) three times, each time raising her hands over my head and lowering them along the sides of my body. Then she tapped lightly on my knee. "You may open your eyes now," she said. "Can you see me clearly? Are you dizzy? Did you feel anything?" To please her, I said that I had had a rather peaceful feeling, as though I had been meditating. (1980:19–20)

This brief scene provides a valuable summary of the principal elements joined in Mahikari. Chanting what to Davis sounded like a Shinto incantation, the practitioner providing the treatment places the patient into a trance. For a Japanese person, this type of chant carries a powerful cultural suggestion for alteration of the state of consciousness, for Shinto rituals all aim at trance induction, misinterpreted in English translations of Japanese texts on Shinto as "alteration of mood." Since meditation is also practiced at some of the services, Davis's answer was not entirely out of place. One cannot expect the correct reaction from a *gaijin* ("foreigner"). Committed to the missionizing goals of her group, she continued with the healing ritual.

The chant the young woman sang following the incantation addressed the spirits possessing the patients, causing them to be unwell, depressed, or even sick. These spirits are unhappy and are roaming the earth instead of working on their development that would eventually take them into paradise. The person performing the treatment can recognize which spirit is possessing the patient from the way the patient moves:

> "The hands of a person being possessed by a snake spirit move this way." She pressed her hands together and began to make twisting, serpentine motions. "A badger spirit will move like this." She clenched her fists and rolled them together. "A fox goes like this." She intertwined her fingers and moved her hands in small circles. "When we are possessed by a human spirit, such as an ancestral ghost, our hands shake up and down. The spirit of a dead bird moves like this." She flapped her arms pretending they were wings. "When a spirit finally is exorcised and leaves the body, a person's hand or shoulder automatically rises toward the ceiling." (1980:25)

In the group Davis studied, the majority of the possessing spirits were dissatisfied, unhappy, injured grandparents (twenty-nine percent). Characteristic of the important role warriors have played in Japanese history, their ghosts were a close second with twenty-seven percent, more important than parents or siblings (1980:122). Ancestral ghosts might be bothered by mismanagement of the family estate, for instance, but more frequently by even minor infractions of their descendants in the care and attendance of the *butsudan,* the shrine containing the tablets that are the abode of the ancestral spirits. Davis found that during lectures at the center, the speaker always had the undivided attention of the audience when discussing this home shrine.

Dissatisfied ghosts may cause financial reversals or, more important, serious illness, especially cancer or ulcers, and death. The client's well-being depends on the healer's adeptness at the negotiations with the spirit entity. They are told to lose their attachment to the possessed body. That will free them from having to be reborn, a borrowing from Buddhism. Arguments are presented to the spirit to coax it to leave. It is threatened that if it fails to do so, it will eventually end up in hell.

Possessing beings may appear as animal spirits first, for instance as badgers. During "Treatment," such a spirit will tell of its grievances, and once given offerings and talked into mending its ways, it will turn into the human spirit it represented, such as a great-great-grandfather. In that form the spirit, while possessing his descendant, will then thank everyone, tears in his (the possessed person's) eyes, and disappear into the astral world.[7]

In Davis's case, no possessing spirit gave any indication of its presence. But since according to Mahikari belief, everyone is contaminated, the healer performed a simple exorcistic ritual anyway. After the conclusion of the chant, she waited for a few minutes to give the spirit another chance to reveal itself, then ordered it to give peace, to be still. In other words, she pronounced an exorcistic formula. She also passed her hands over Davis's side and back, a cleansing ritual we encountered also among the Spiritualists and Umbandists. Although she knew that she had not succeeded in expelling whatever noxious entity was inhabiting the American sociologist, she graciously treated his back and abdomen, explaining that the "miracles" of healing were brought about by her raising her hands over the diseased parts of the patient's body. That made the spirit rays penetrate them, purifying and expelling the toxins. When people have convulsions during such treatment, that is believed to be the noxious spirits moving inside.

Once converted or dispatched to the higher regions, the previously harmful spirits may decide to help their former victims instead. The Nakayama center was set up by its founder to honor his father, whose spirit had caused illness and even death in the family. But once satisfied with the treatment at the hands of its descendants, the spirit declared, "You have found a wonderful *kami*," and started helping them. The family stayed well, it prospered, and so did the center.

Before we leave the topic of Japanese possession, a comparison with Spiritualism and Umbanda may be in order. The difference between the spirit entities involved is quite clear. But we are also struck by the relatively minor role of the healers. Aside from inducing the trance in the patient, their only "nonordinary" activity is the transmission of the "spirit rays" that have curative powers, in some respects similar to the "influences" of Spiritualism and the "fluids" of Umbanda. While in those two religions it is the medium that is possessed and the spirits help the client, here we find a double inversion. Not only are the spirits rarely helpful, they do not possess the healer, either. Rather, it is the patient who experiences possession, and the cure consists of expelling the spirit. Numerous New Religions of Japan are similar to Mahikari in this respect, so we may expect to find some basis in folklore. And indeed, there is a folk tradition called *yorigitō* that may well account for the agreement.

Yorigitō is a village ritual for establishing contact with the spirit world involving two practitioners, a medium *(miko)* and an ascetic. The medium is entirely passive. It is the ascetic who induces the trance in the medium by reciting sutras and chanting invocatory formulas. He then calls the spirit into the medium, interrogates it while it is thus accessible, and sends it back home again. The ritual was brought to Japan in the ninth century from China, where it was borrowed in turn from India.[8] There it was originally used in order to petition a deity to possess the body of a child, whereupon it could be asked questions of importance to the community or to the petitioner, often a ruler. Presumably the beneficent deity left on its own accord upon conclusion of the ritual. It is when the possessing spirit is of a lower order, a neglected ghost or a spirit fox, for instance, that trouble or illness results. Such a spirit will not leave voluntarily. It needs to be cajoled into leaving the body of the victim and entering a medium. While there, it can then be interrogated, asked about its motive, forced to name itself, and, with luck, dispatched to where it came from.

Although *yorigitō* is nowadays relegated to the most isolated villages of Japan, it is still the basis for exorcising unwanted spirit entities in the New Religions of today, although in a somewhat contracted form. In Mahikari and elsewhere, the patients themselves act as mediums, while the healer providing the treatment assumes the role of the ascetic.

6 THE MULTIPLE PERSONALITY EXPERIENCE AND DEMONIC POSSESSION

The multiple personality experience or "disorder" is not usually covered in discussions of demonic possession. That is regrettable, for as we saw in chapter 1, there is a lot that it can teach us about possession, and it also offers some insights into its demonic variant. Perhaps because the multiple personality syndrome is relatively rare, authors of texts on comparative religion are usually not even aware of its existence and would disregard it anyhow, because of the prevailing view that it is exclusively a psychiatric problem.[1]

Briefly, as will be remembered from chapter 1 and the case of Eve White, patients suffering from this condition experience themselves as having several discrete personalities called alternates that do not share consciousness or memories with their host. That means that the host does not know or is not able to recall what the various alternate personalities do, and extended periods of amnesia, often starting during childhood, are characteristically reported by these patients. Each one of the alternates has its own complex social patterns and behavior. When a given personality is dominant, it will control the individual's behavior. As should be obvious by now, this description could just as well be cited in any discussion of the experience of possession. There are, however, in the main two differences between this disorder and possession as a religious experience. One of these concerns how the phenomenon is located culturally, that is, what society, especially those charged with treating the patient, thinks is going on. The other is the nature of the beings involved in the possession.

The multiple personality disorder, as mentioned before, is reported to be rare. It was earlier held that it was mainly an ailment afflicting women, but in tune with our present cultural changes, therapists have taken a second look and now believe that this impression may be a result of sampling bias. In other words, with the diagnostician expecting to see the multiple personality problem in female patients, he may not recognize the same complaint in a man, and the male population would therefore probably be underrepresented in statistical studies. In the past, the affliction was frequently not identified correctly, and cases were misdiagnosed as depression, schizophrenia, epilepsy, or hysterical neurosis, or were simply viewed as clever role playing, and thus remained unreported. For unknown reasons, and we will come back to this observation later, an unusually large number of cases appeared in the decade of the seventies.

Because health professionals were beginning to see more patients with the complaint and had more data to go on, there was a growing realization that, indeed, this was a separate diagnostic entity. Upon the insistence of psychiatrists treating such patients and against much opposition, the authoritative DSM-III, the *Diagnostic and Statistical Manual of Mental Disorders,* 3d ed. (1980), finally recognized the multiple personality syndrome as a separate, chronic dissociative disorder. Dissociation is here understood in this context to be a psychophysiological process during which there is a disturbance in a person's sense of self-identity and memory.

There are various theories about the causes for the condition. Prevailing thinking is based on the observation, well supported by recent studies of as many as one hundred instances,[2] that the overwhelming majority of individuals showing the multiple personality disturbance have been sexually and/or physically abused as children. That, according to Putnam,[3] prompts various alternate personalities to "split off" from the core of the self. As we notice, the experience is not interpreted in religious terms. The distinct personalities joined in the patient do not originate from outside the person, in another reality, which would be the interpretation in the terms of the "soul theory," but come about by forces or experiences internal to the individual. The entities in question are not spirits in this view, they are "alters."

As to the nature of the alternate personalities, the alter may be of the opposite sex and/or of a life style very different from that of the host personality. Clinicians frequently see personality types that have a definite function to perform in the patient's life.[4] There is a child personality buffering traumatic experiences, and there are "Inner Self Helpers."[5] In contrast to these kindly entities, at least one of the alternate personalities present is usually noxious to varying degrees. A patient whose case was reported by Edward W. Beal[6] had one among her three personalities called Marie, who was "insensitive, hostile, overly suspicious and overbearing." Others[7] found alters that were cold, belligerent, sullen, and "scary to interview," and experienced therapists warn that psychiatrists must be wary and can expect violence on the part of the patient when such alters are "out." In addition, multiples also experience persecutors who inflict punishment, often in the form of self-mutilation or suicide. The latter is sometimes a criminal, and murderous, evil personality. In other words, the entities appearing in such a person may be kindly, dangerous, or even demonic.

The multiple personality syndrome was not recognized in Europe as a separate clinical entity until the 1700s, when descriptions of it began appearing in the medical literature. The question we need to ask is, why at this particular time in European history? The reason is that this was the era that marked the advent of the Age of Enlightenment. One of the features characterizing the age was that the cities became emancipated from agriculturalist traditions, and thinkers were no longer constrained to interpret everything they observed in religious terms.

We might be tempted to argue that it must then have been the life style of the city that brought about this form of personality problem. But if it were city living that produced the condition, many people would show up with it, as they do, for instance, with stress-related illnesses, which are recognized as being associated with life in the modern city. But instead the multiple personality disorder is quite rare; it simply crops up here and there, seemingly without any pattern. Neither can researchers show that a majority of adults who were abused as children will later become multiples. Instead, multiples have usually been abused as children, which is an entirely different matter, meaning that abuse has been a contributing factor. So where does that leave us?

Let us recall here what we suggested in chapter 1, namely, that the ability to enter into the religious trance, to experience ecstasy, was an inherited trait, and that this might be true also of the ability to switch brain maps. If this trait is heritable, it must have been with us from very early times in our cultural evolution, and just as in the case of the religious trance, we would assume, our antecedents learned in the course of millennia to control this very special capability ritually, as we saw in the various possession ceremonies, so that it could be used for important religious and social ends. With the help of the trance, a new map could be called forth, and then it could be wiped away again.

But what happens to a genetic endowment that is no longer needed culturally? It does not, of course, simply go away. It will continue being available, and people will accidentally stray into it, just as they do into trance. That can happen especially, as the research referred to above shows, if a person has been severely abused, the personality structure has been damaged, the integrity of the person has been violated, as happens in child abuse.

A remark repeated by several authors almost as an aside lends added support to this line of argument: "For unknown reasons," they write, cases suddenly multiplied in the 1970s. Actually, however, the reasons for that increase are not difficult to understand if we remember that in all *ritually* controlled possession cases, it is the religious trance that mediates the experience. The body is readied for possession by the changes that take place as the trance is induced. In the 1960s and continuing into the early part of the 1970s, during the time of the youth movement and the counterculture, many more people than ever before experimented with various altered states. It will be remembered that trance is also involved when a personality of a multiple personality patient "comes out." So it is simply a matter of statistical probability that with more people experiencing the religious trance, and brain map flipping or exchanging being a genetic ability, some of these subjects would stray into the disorder of the multiple personality experience. Unfortunately for them, however, the rituals for handling this genetic endowment safely are no longer known in the city. So once caught up in the behavior of relinquishing their personality map and instituting another, people have no idea about how to undo what came about without their conscious knowledge or intention, and there is no specialist with the requisite information to whom they could safely turn. The patient in that case is much like the princess of old whom a sorcerer has locked into a tower. She may cry at the tower window, but no suitor can free her unless someone gives him the key to the door.

With the therapists at a loss as to how to help their patients, practically all the individual cases known from the literature have a feeling of tragic inescapability about them. There was the famous Miss Beauchamp, described in 1906 by Morton Prince, a respected neurologist. He became well known for talking at length about her:

> She had individual peculiarities of character, of disposition, of temperament, of tastes, of habits, of memory, and of physical health, which sharply distinguished her from B. I. (another personality). Even many of her physiological reactions to the environment were different.[8]

He examined her, he wrote about her, but when all was said and done, he could not help her, and she had to continue living with her frightening problem. Or remember Eve White from *The Three Faces of Eve* (chap. 1). Dr. Thigpen's efforts did not free her of her bothersome alternate personality. On the contrary, she eventually ended up with sixteen different alters, as though all that had been accomplished was a "shattering" of the original alternate brain map.[9]

Usually, not much is known about the subsequent fate of multiples, once they no longer visit their psychiatrists. But there is one report in the literature about a woman whose case was followed for thirty-eight years.[10] In the course of such a long time, a number of different treatments were tried, some initially under the erroneous assumption that she suffered from schizophrenia. She was treated with hypnosis and given supportive psychotherapy, as well as classical and modified psychoanalysis. But the authors of the report come to the dispirited conclusion that even if such modern therapeutic approaches had been available to her from the start, the outcome would not have been any different: she would still be a multiple.

Other pitiable sufferers were subjected to insulin or electroconvulsive shock, and to psychoactive medication, as well as to attempts at trying to "fuse" their distinct personalities into a new, integrated persona. Although some psychiatrists report successful fusions, none of this has proved generally and reliably effective. The most that can be hoped for under present regimens is to make the patient more relaxed and accepting of his/her condition, and thus more capable of coping with it and, in effect, hiding it from public view.

What happens, however, if one of the alters is evil and commits murder and mayhem without the host being aware of it, or having any memory of it at all? Neither Miss Beauchamp nor Eve White had any criminal alters. But the contention that the crime was committed while the offender was possessed by a demon keeps cropping up as a defense in criminal court cases. And the literature contains records of a number of famous killers who maintained until the day of their execution that they were innocent of the crimes they had been convicted of and that they had absolutely no memory of having committed any of it. Were the hosts in these instances in fact innocent, and were they killed by the state for the crimes of their alters?

A famous example of a criminal alternate personality, although the man was not later executed, is that of "Killer Burke," one of the men responsible for the gang slaying that has gone down in history as the St. Valentine's Day Massacre.[11] Burke was the son of a farming family, and was perfectly normal until he was twenty-four years old. Without any known provocation, he unexpectedly left home and lived for six months as a dangerous, violent tramp. He returned home, once more the man he had been before this episode, married, and lived an ordinary, respectable life for four years, when another emergence of his alter took him to Chicago. He became a feared gangster, and in 1929, on St. Valentine's Day, he and some associates went to a garage where a number of rival mobsters were assembled, and mowed them down with machine-gun fire. The police arrived too late to arrest the murderers, and Burke went home to his wife, not remembering anything of the event and knowing only that he had been to Chicago to look for work.

For years, Burke went on alternating between a pleasant, hardworking husband and father and a vicious murderer, eventually killing possibly as many as thirty-two people. He was finally caught when, while living as a respected businessman in a city in Michigan, he was stopped because of a minor traffic accident. Instead of calmly answering the officer's questions, his criminal alter suddenly took over, and he started shooting. As the mortally wounded officer put it, he "turned into a demon." He was sentenced to life imprisonment, and although he was a model prisoner, even his fellow inmates were terrified of him, because his murderous alter could spring into action without warning. Until the end of his days, he remained a multiple.

While Western-type psychiatric and biomedical treatment of the condition often remains ineffective, it seems that at least in some cases exorcism works promptly and well. What sets these cases apart, according to the observations of the California psychiatrist Ralph B. Allison,[12] are certain characteristics of the alternate personalities themselves. He contends that under ordinary circumstances, alternate personalities arise and serve a definite and practical purpose. An alter "is a means of coping with an emotion or situation that the patient cannot handle" (1980:184). Sometimes it is difficult to discover what that original purpose was, but eventually, the psychiatrist can pinpoint both the cause and the time or situation in a patient's life when the "birth" of such an alternate took place. Treatment aims at teaching the patient alternate coping strategies, which then ideally would mean that the alters would dissolve. But aside from the fact that in his experience this hoped-for resolution did not always come about, Allison also occasionally came across entities in his work with multiples that acted anomalously. Their "birth" could not be pinpointed, they served no recognizable purpose, and quite frequently they referred to themselves as spirits. They were not always absolutely evil. In one case a male being calling itself Dennis appeared seemingly out of nowhere and then refused to leave because it had fallen in love with one of the alters of Allison's patient. The entity was not demonic, just bothersome. But in the case of Carrie, a multiple patient Allison had treated for years, a truly furious possession took place suddenly and without warning, exhibiting some of the traits of demonic possession we will discuss later (see chap. 8); the alter screamed obscenities, had superhuman strength, and was viciously aggressive. Before Allison could help, Carrie committed suicide. People suffering from demonic possession often report that the demon wants to kill them by forcing them into a suicidal act. In this instance, it happened.

Allison felt that if these alters pretended to be or actually were spirits, it might do his patients no harm if he tried an exorcism. It seemed a matter of logic then to find out what the ritual of exorcism consisted of in the often-quoted biblical stories. Using a strategy patterned on those ancient reports, he was actually able to cure a number of such patients whose alters fitted the picture. It certainly worked in the instance mentioned above with the spirit called Dennis. In one case, he also enlisted the help of a religious specialist:[13]

> I once saw a young man who had been injured at work when a piece of machinery fell on his head. He had had several subsequent convulsive seizures but neurological evaluations did not show injury sufficient to explain the seizures. He also began hearing a voice telling him he was going to die shortly. Under hypnosis, I asked to learn the reason for these symptoms. A voice came forth, claiming to be the Devil. This Devil claimed to have entered the man several years before, when he was in Japan in the U.S. Army. The man had run into a burning house to rescue a Japanese occupant and, when he did, an explosion blew him out of the house. The man was hospitalized for many months. . . . This Devil claimed he went into the man at the time of the fire and was responsible for all subsequent physical and mental symptoms. I secured a consultation with a local priest, who also met this same Devil, just by reciting certain rituals. The priest expressed an opinion that this was really not the Devil, as known in theology, but that he was an evil spirit who was so stupid that he actually thought he was the Devil.

The priest then carried out an exorcism, and it was so successful that according to Allison, who continued to correspond with the patient, "the symptoms of the voice and seizures did not continue after he left the priest."

As an aside, knowing what we do about the dangerous spirits making life miserable for some people in Japan, it is amusing to learn that the priest found that the possessing spirit who invaded the man in Japan was not "the real Devil, as known in [Christian] theology," but rather a stupid spirit who pretended to be the Devil. Did the spirit assume this disguise for added prestige and credibility in California, where mere Japanese spirits would not carry much weight? At any rate, the important matter is the successful and rather uncomplicated resolution of the multiple personality disorder of this serviceman by the use of the ritual of exorcism.

To my knowledge, there are unfortunately not many psychiatrists faced with the multiple personality disorder in their patients willing to try exorcism or at least to enlist the services of an exorcist. That is too bad, because exorcism is basically designed to help the afflicted person to gain ritual control over the molesting entities, and quite possibly it would work whether those beings declare themselves to be spirits or not. Thinking back on the experiences that are common knowledge especially in Umbanda, unruly spirits need to and indeed can be trained.

The multiple personality disorder conveniently introduces us to the topic of demonic possession. It allows us to examine a genetic ability in the raw, as it were, as an urban phenomenon unencumbered by religious context. People apparently have the ability under certain circumstances to switch or create new brain maps, in the city obviously adapted to the needs of psychological survival. Beings or alters of many different shadings may appear. But without ritual intervention, the undoing of such a pattern is extremely difficult, especially so if the alter is evil or, in religious terms, if the possessing entity has demonic powers. In the religious ambient, the treatment of choice is exorcism. As we shall see, it is the only strategy used cross-culturally against demonic possession, and in all instances where it is allowed to work without interference, it is eminently successful.

7 THE GHOSTS THAT KILL

While the multiple personality disorder is rarely interpreted as a condition of demonic possession (although in some instances, as we saw, that would certainly be appropriate), in other contexts the term is bandied about with considerable bravado. In the opening speeches at a newly founded Christian Center for Information about the Occult in Santa Fe, New Mexico, in 1985, everything popularly subsumed under New Age, such as astrology, aura balancing, crystal healing, plus anything having to do with Spiritualism, was classified as demonic possession. The speakers at this center were fundamentalist Protestants, but when it comes to indicting Satan for the supposed ills of the age, Catholic popular writers do not lag far behind. A Viennese author writing in 1976[1] includes all the above, while adding also black magic, satanic cults, divination, and spirit journeys to the list. In a 1985 television interview, a Pentecostal minister advocated exorcism for gays, which thus by implication is also classified as possession by an evil spirit. It seems that even in this supposedly rational and scientific modern age, there is no dearth of those who will summarily accuse people of being possessed by abominable spirits if they succumb to the allure of anything culturally decried or censured at the time. But the spirits called up under such circumstances seem rather anemic as devils go. Upon closer examination, they turn out to be no more than flimsy masks used to give an aura of authority to a parochial, dogmatically informed judgment: "In a manner of speaking," if I see a certain behavior, such as people wearing a crystal on a necklace or paying for an astrological chart, I should warn them in Christian charity that Satan is close by, tempting them to commit an act that within our doctrine, which represents the only Truth, is a Sin. The Evil One, in fact, may have already taken possession of them, and poor benighted ones, they do not even realize it.

True demonic possession is something totally different. To make that clear, let us recall here first how illness and the relationship to the spirits were conceptualized and experienced in the various possession cults we described before.

1. Those who experienced possession by kindly, positive, helpful beings, the Spiritualists, Umbandists, and Pentecostals (chaps. 2–4), saw no direct relationship between their spirits and that which might ail them. The spirits were not the cause of their illnesses and their troubles. Instead, they were helpful in restoring health and happiness. Simultaneously, the hosts of the spirits enjoyed near-total autonomy: the possessing entity needed to wait until it was invited and had to leave when it became time to do so. In fact, in some instances, such as with the Spiritualists and to a lesser extent with the Umbandists, the hosts were even able to choose which of the spirits was to have the privilege of borrowing their bodies for a while.

2. In the Japanese possession religions, the situation was somewhat different, in the sense that the spirits caused the illness and the trouble. That happened not because they were intrinsically malevolent, or spirits of dead, of the ancestors. Spirits of animals could also be responsible for the affliction. They caused problems because whether animal or human, they were unhappy, neglected ghosts. People had an interest in keeping spirits happy, and could do so by fulfilling their ritual duties, such as, for instance, caring for the ancestral shrine in the proper manner. So they actually had some choice in the matter of their own welfare. Naturally, they could still become ill, for some despondent spirit could enter uninvited. Once such a being was ensconced, it did not leave on its own accord, and quite a bit of effort was needed in order to dislodge or exorcize it. But there was no one particular physical ill caused by demons. They were blamed for any illness and difficulty, and their attack, although a worrisome matter, could be warded off by relatively mild exorcistic measures.

By contrast, demonic possession is a frightening, negative experience of some uninvited evil entities assuming complete control over one's body. To be sure, even in this case they cannot arbitrarily take over anybody's body. A malevolent action, an aggression of some kind, must first create a breach in a person's natural defenses. But once the demons have entered, they pose a threat of catastrophic dimensions.

If we compare cases of such demonic possession cross-culturally, we find that the possession originating in the large agricultural societies of Africa differs in its general characteristics from the one of Eurasian provenience. There is, in fact, a demonic possession of the African type, and another one of the Eurasian type. This is a matter not of genetic disposition but of cultural ambient. Adolf Rodewyk[2] mentions a case of two black girls working in the home of German missionaries in Africa. Both experienced the Eurasian and not the African type of possession. In the following, we will treat these variants separately, with the topic of the present chapter being the African type of demonic possession.

The agriculturalist societies of Africa have richly developed positive possession complexes used especially for healing and divining; in addition, they also serve to reinforce social control and to provide the powerless with a measure of influence, as well as help to meet other, diverse social needs, depending on the particular cultural situation. The possessing spirits are in this case benevolent, helpful entities, and the relationship between spirits and humans is one of reciprocity: Humans keep the spirits alive by offering them sacrifices and allowing them to participate in the social process by lending them their bodies. Such kindly spirits appear only when invited, and never in association with any evil entity.

Some spiritual beings, however, specifically ghosts, that is, spirits of the dead, permit themselves to be misused for evil ends, for sorcery. What Elizabeth Colson, an American anthropologist who did field-work in Central Africa, says about the Tonga ghosts holds true for Sub-Saharan Africa generally:

> Ghost possession [is] wholly undesirable. Victim and helpers seek only to expel a ghost and prevent its re-entry. The ghost has no message to give, either public or private; it has no desire to be appeased. Ghosts have no mediums, only victims, and these must be short-term ones; either a ghost is expelled or the victim dies. (1969:72)

This straightforward, tremendously threatening but also relatively simple, and therefore probably ancient form of demonic possession was carried to the Western Hemisphere by African slaves, and today can be encountered in all those regions where they originally settled.

Let us once more turn to *vodun* in order to understand what is involved. In the *vodun* religion, demonic possession is the result of sorcery, and the spirits involved are spirits of the dead. Such possession results in the afflicted growing thin, spitting blood, and soon dying. As Alfred Métraux, the French anthropologist and well-known expert on Haitian *vodun* quoted also in chapter 1,[3] describes it, the person who wants to kill someone by sending the dead against him appeals to the god Saint Expédit by uttering a prayer before his image, which has been placed upside down. In this prayer the supplicant promises to take Saint Expédit as his patron from that day on. He asks him to rid him of his adversary: "Rid me of his head, rid me of his memory, rid me of his thought, rid me of his house. . . ."

The curse will not become effective, however, unless the good will of the all-powerful master of the dead, Baron-Samedi, has also been enlisted. To this end the sorcerer strikes his machete three times against a stone dedicated to this god, and with each blow utters the god's name. He then becomes possessed by Baron-Samedi, who speaks through his mouth and orders him to go to the cemetery at midnight:

> There [he must] offer bananas and potatoes, chopped small, in front of the cross which symbolizes him. There too he must take a handful of earth for each of the 'dead' whom he wishes to send and must spread it on some path frequently taken by his victim. Whether the unfortunate man shall step on or step over the earth makes little difference: the dead will enter his body and hold him close for ever. (1959:275)

To rid a person of these malevolent spirits of the dead is extremely difficult, because they embed themselves in the patient's organism. Métraux witnessed an exorcism of this kind, carried out for a man named Antoine, who a few weeks earlier had been a sturdy stevedore on the Port-au-Prince docks. Suddenly, he had become ill, wasting away at an alarming rate. The treatment by an *houngan* was unsuccessful, and the man became despondent and could not even swallow food any more. His alarmed family then took him to Lorgina, a *mambo* or priestess, who undertook the cure because Brisé, her own *loa,* had promised his full cooperation.

Lorgina had determined by divination that Antoine was possessed by three "dead." In view of the nature and severity of his illness, the treatment was carried out in the house reserved for the spirits of death, the Guédé. Their signs had been traced on the floor in ashes and coffee grounds, and the patient's mat was placed on top of this design. A table was set with the stone of the *loa* Brisé; there were also five bunches of leaves and three calabashes containing maize and grilled peanuts, a candle in each one. Two troughs under the table contained a "bath" of plants soaking in water with bull's bile.

The patient was carried in and placed on the mat. On the way in, the "dead" inside him continually defied the *mambo,* swearing that they would not let her drive them out. Antoine was stripped down to his pants and then laid out and prepared as though he were a corpse: his jaw was bound with a strip of material, his nostrils were closed with small wads of cotton, his arms were crossed, and his big toes were tied together. Small piles of peanuts and maize were arranged on his palms, forehead, chest, and stomach.

Lorgina next brought a hen and a rooster and invoked the spirits. An assistant took the fowl to the patient and had them peck at each pile of food, beginning at the head. When the rooster refused to eat of the grain, another one was brought, which pecked eagerly. The birds were then placed on the patient, two on his chest and one between his legs. Meanwhile, Lorgina knelt down and started praying, reciting invocations to Saint Expédit, the *loas*, and a long series of Credos, Ave Marias, and the Lord's Prayer, always beginning with, "In the name of God the Father, God the Son, and God the Holy Ghost, in the name of Mary, in the name of Jesus and all the Saints and all the dead."

She then got up and began passing the hen and the rooster over the body of the patient, starting at his head and reciting incantations, such as, "All that is bad is to come out, all that is good is to go in." Both she and her assistant made little hissing sounds like those of the snake god Damballah. The assistant repeated the passing of the fowl over the patient, who began to tremble at this point, but was cautioned by the *mambo* to keep still. She started invoking all her own *loas*, as well as the ancestors and the *loa* of Antoine, asking them to save him and make him well. The hen and the rooster were passed over him one last time, and were left dazed by his side.

The ritual continued with the three calabashes and then Brisé's stone being passed over the patient. The *mambo* then took some of the "bath" into her cupped hands and threw it into the face of the patient. He trembled, shuddered, grunted, and tried to get up, but was re-strained. Relatives of the afflicted man who had come to help and watch could hardly stand the brutality with which he was being treated, and one girl, in tears, wanted to leave but was ordered to stay. Lorgina explained to Antoine that the dead were moving inside him and disturbing him. Some of those present began helping with the "bath," producing a continuous shower of decaying leaves and bile water over the patient's face and chest, offensive to the "dead" and designed to drive them out. Lorgina kept threatening the "dead" and ordering them out. The patient's movements became more and more violent, until he actually threw off his bonds and chin strip.

Finally the man fell back on his mat in total exhaustion, and Lorgina called him by his name: "Antoine, Antoine, is it you there?" He answered with a faint "Yes," whereupon the assistant set fire to some raw rum around Brisé's stone, scooped up the flames with his hands, and ran them all over the patient. Lorgina took rum in her mouth and squirted it roughly into his face. When he tried to protect his eyes, he was once more restrained. This part of the treatment was brought to an end by an assistant rubbing him and pummeling him with the edge of her hands on his shoulders, the bend of his arms, and under his knees.

The second part of the ritual was carried out in the yard, where a ditch had been dug. It was surrounded by three calabashes and seven "eternal" orange-peel lamps burning brightly. The patient was placed into the ditch and handed a small banana tree, which had been uprooted for this purpose, and which he embraced. The hen was brought out and passed over his body, while Lorgina recited a lengthy exorcistic formula, calling on God, the saints, various *loas*, and the spirits of death to give life back to the patient. She had paid cash for that; "I paid you, I owe you nothing." She then took the contents of the calabashes, rubbed the patient down with it, and, taking a pitcher full of water, poured its contents over him and broke it. She anointed his body with the oil from the lamps and then helped him to rise. The hen was placed among the roots of the palm, and the trench was quickly filled, burying the hen alive, and the earth smoothed. Only three of the eternal lamps marked the spot.

In conclusion, the patient was rubbed down with flaming rum, and to rout the "dead" once and for all, three small charges were set off between his legs. Lorgina and her assistants squirted rum over him and blew some of it into the four cardinal directions, to the cracking of a special *petro* whip. A white shirt edged in red was brought out. Lorgina burned a corner of it, made some marks with the blackened section on Antoine's face and chest, then helped him put it on. He was instructed to spit a lot, his feet were washed in an herbal decoction, and he was given some tea to drink. The banana tree eventually died, indicating that Baron-Samedi had accepted the hen in payment for Antoine's life. And indeed, his recovery was nothing short of miraculous. He began eating again, and soon he had gained back enough strength that he was able to resume work as a stevedore.

How this remarkable treatment was able completely to reverse the deadly spiral that Antoine was caught in becomes understandable if we realize that what Lorgina used was a powerful and extremely ancient ritual. As I showed elsewhere,[4] ceremonies of this structure were current around the world in hunter-gatherer societies and can still be witnessed there. As a mode of curing, the rite passed down to African agriculturalists through the millennia, and it is truly remarkable that it should have been preserved in Haiti in such admirably pure and complete form. In the ritual, the patient was subjected to an enactment of death and rebirth, complete with reducing him to a corpse, burying him, and then having him be born from the depth of the ditch-womb, and finally giving him his first bath and making him drink like a newborn infant. The effect of the powerful drama was reinforced on the neurophysiological level, because with its help, Lorgina efficiently induced the trance, as evidenced by the trembling of the patient and the protestations of the possessing ghosts. As a result, she was able to blot out the lethal brain map and to return Antoine to his former healthy identity.

Not all Haitian demonic possession cases need to be treated with a complete ritual of the sort that Antoine underwent. Métraux describes abbreviated forms, successful under less severe conditions, and Stephen D. Glazier, an American anthropologist, observed such short exorcisms in the 1970s also in Trinidad, which, moreover, represented an extensively syncretized form of the African original.[5] On that island, demonic possession is part of the native belief concerning *obeahmen*. These individuals are believed to have the power to cast demons into others in order to make them ill or to kill them. They work under orders of someone who wishes the victim's death, and the demon can be removed only by another, even more powerful *obeahman*. Since such treatments are expensive, victims frequently seek help from various syncretic cults, such as Xango or Rada, but also from Christian denominations, from Catholic priests, and particularly from the Pentecostals, where exorcism is a regular feature of the services. The following is that part of Glazier's description of such a service which concerns exorcism:

> The services are performed twice a week. Wednesday exorcisms begin at nine o'clock in the morning and last most of the day, while Friday service begins in the evening and goes well into the night. During the first two hours of service, recorded music is played and those who desire to receive the Holy Spirit are organized into one long line to pass before the altar. The pastor blesses each person practicing the laying on of hands. At this time, those possessed by demons begin to quake and shout; they must be restrained and returned to their seats. Of the hundreds who pass before the altar, only a few (five or six) are found to be victims of *obeah* attack. [The rest are understood to have medical problems and are encouraged to consult the nurse of the congregation or a physician.] Rites of exorcism are not performed until the final hours of the service. . . . [The pastor] turns to the congregation and tells them that they must praise the Lord for what they have heard here today [during testimonies]. The congregation responds by standing, raising their hands in the air, and chanting: "Praise the Lord . . . Jesus . . . Jesus . . . Praise the Lord . . . Jesus . . . Jesus!" The emotion builds as the pastor reminds the congregation that demons cannot bear to hear the holy name of Jesus. . . . The possessed jump from their seats screaming. Church helpers rush to wherever they are and carry them to the front of the church. Usually one or two new victims are discovered at this time.
>
> The pastor approaches each victim individually. He brings the hand microphone down from the altar so that all may hear the possessed. This adds considerably to the dramatic impact of exorcism. He asks four questions of each victim: 1) who sent you? 2) how many are you?

3) why are you in him? and 4) how long have you been in him? The
response is a series of shrieks and garbled curses.

When the demons do not respond to the pastor's questions co-
herently, he pretends to lose his patience. The exchanges between the
pastor and the demons are often humorous, taking on an element of
play. . . .

Pastor: "I don't have any more time to waste on you, you filthy little
demon! Get out!"

Demon: "Ahhggg . . . I want to kill her."

Pastor: "Why do you want to kill this sweet thing?"

Demon: "Ahhggg . . . (unclear curses)."

Pastor: All right . . . I'll give you to the count of five to leave . . . one
. . . two. . . ."

Here is another example:

Pastor: "Why are you in her?"

Demon: "Ahhggg . . . I hate her!

Pastor: "Why do you hate her?"

Demon: "She snores! . . . Ahhggg!"

After five or ten minutes of banter with the demons, the pastor grabs
the victim by the throat and commands the demon to leave 'in the
name of Jesus.' The victim gags; this is taken as a sign of the demon's
departure. Some victims are found to be possessed by twenty demons
or more. (pp. 4–5)

If we compare this ritual with what we saw in *vodun* above, we find
that the element of sorcery is still in place, as is the disastrous effect of
the possession. The rough handling of the victim is also familiar. But
the fact of the spontaneous revelation of the demon's presence during
a prayer for the Holy Spirit is new, as is the questioning of the demon
by the pastor. These are elements added from the Eurasian type,
which we shall discuss next.

8   LEGION OF DEMONS

In addition to the African variant of demonic possession, there are innumerable stories also of another type, which we will here call the Eurasian variant, because it is reported from India and China, as well as from Christian Europe. In a number of characteristics this Eurasian form of possession agrees with its African counterpart. In both, the noxious spirit entities invade their victim uninvited, but have to wait until a path opens for them, a breach of sorts in the personality of their intended victim. Their presence is signaled by illness. If a trance is ritually initiated, the spirits reveal their presence. Healing is accomplished by dislodging, expelling, that is, exorcising, the malevolent being.

But differences emerge all along the line, with the African variant in each instance simpler and at the same time much more sinister, which confirms its greater antiquity. In the African variant, the invaders are always ghosts. In Eurasia, on the other hand, there is a great variety of such evil beings. According to European folk belief, for instance, also fervently held by Protestant fundamentalists in this country, there is a whole slew of demons, associated with Satan as his entourage, fallen angels and unredeemed humans, roaming the earth, eager to possess, corrupt, and plague humanity. In the Christian West, the principal guardian of the tradition about demons is the Catholic church. According to a contemporary catechism,[1] devils or demons represent temptation, confusion, deception; they are inimical to humans, barring their entrance to heaven.

In both types of possession, the condition of being possessed by demons is recognized by outward signs. In *vodun* the presence of the "dead" was signaled by a single, acute, and devastating illness. In the Eurasian type, there is a chronic phase of depression and frightening visions, interspersed with individual episodes of violent possession, often described as attacks. These have a clearly marked onset, where the subject visibly slips into a religious trance, and which is characterized by intractable raging. In addition, for the Eurasian type, there are a number of typical symptoms of possession. When in the Catholic church permission is asked of the bishop for the performance of the grand ritual of exorcism, the "test" involves a determination whether a well-known set of these symptoms has been identified, mainly whether the demon has taken over the body of the victim, indicated by violent aversion to everything sacred, and whether it speaks from the victim's mouth. In addition, there are a number of typical neurophysiological and psychological signs that indicate demonic possession, although not all of them are present in every case. These include:

insomnia;

fever;

agitation;

roaming;

compusively eating strange or repulsive substances, or refusing all food, resulting in an anorexialike condition;

repulsive stench;

copious foaming saliva;

trembling, which may escalate into convulsions;

rigidity of muscles up to a catatonialike state;

severe abdominal pain;

screaming fits;

grinding of teeth;

uncontrollable weeping;

superhuman strength;

a near-total change in facial features;

a number of different forms of aggression, especially autoaggression up to suicide and aggression against associates;

the demons speak with a rasping, low voice completely unlike that of the natural voice of the speaker, often switching into

corprolalia (uttering strings of insults and obscenities) in combination with copious divinatory or prophetic pronouncements.

The latter phenomenon, namely, that demons first of all utter obscenities and, second, often have things to say that are highly significant within the respective cultural scene, is one of the most striking features of Eurasian demonic possession, and one, therefore, that is often reported. Justinus Kerner, an early-nineteenth-century

German physician and a pioneer in the modern study of possession, cites a story from the sixteenth century:

> The latter [a girl] was possessed by the demon who often threw her to the ground as if she had the falling sickness. Soon the demon began to speak with her mouth and said things inhuman and marvellous which may not be repeated. . . . All the priests of the place and from roundabout came and spoke to her, but the devil replied to them with a contempt which exceeded all bounds, and when he was questioned about Jesus he made a reply of such derision that it cannot be set down.[2]

The propensity of demons for spouting words both "inhuman and marvellous" would obviously invite cultural utilization.[3] The way this happened was to argue that what demons approved of must be evil; what they attacked must be praiseworthy; and what they said under duress, especially under orders from the Virgin Mary, could be quoted as deriving from the highest authority. Thus, in Europe in the not-so-distant past, what demons said speaking from the mouth of the possessed quickly made the rounds and carried as much weight as nowadays remarks of a powerful politician at a press conference. Demonic pronouncements were suitable and versatile weapons in inner-church conflicts, theological controversies, and church politics. In the sixteenth and seventeenth centuries, for instance, utterances of demons were applied promiscuously in the struggle of the Catholic church against the Lutherans. At the beginning of the nineteenth, the demons gave voice within the Catholic church to the opposition to reform movements deemed too rationalistic. The demons of Anneliese Michel, the German university student whose case was mentioned in the Introduction, had much to say concerning the reforms introduced by the Second Ecumenical Council: They heartily approved of them. Today, ten years after her death, this material is still circulating widely in the more traditionally oriented Catholic underground, not only in the German-speaking parts of Europe but apparently in this country, as well. After the publication in 1981 of my book about the case in this country, I received a letter from a woman who, she wrote, had heard that Anneliese's demons had mentioned something about Father Lefebvre, a French priest opposed to the reforms instituted after the Second Ecumenical Council, and what exactly had the demons said about him?

There are differences between the African and the Eurasian types also with respect to the reasons why evil beings invade a person. The *vodun* "dead" were passive, misused in the service of sorcery. Evil spirits in the Eurasian variant of demonic possession invade because they are intrinsically and actively the enemies of humans. All they need is an entranceway into their prospective victim provided by sorcery or witchcraft, or by a curse. The breaking of a powerful taboo or committing of a serious crime may also open the door to demonic forces. Once a victim is in serious danger, he/she will have visions of the evil beings hovering about. Another important difference between the two variants is the fact that in the Eurasian type the demons have personal characteristics, although no redeeming qualities; they are not undifferentiated ghosts. And as beings of deception, they tempt humans into actions socially unacceptable and decried, that is, culturally threatening at the particular time and place.

Once evil entities have settled in, they hang on for dear life, tormenting their victims and trying to kill them. So it becomes imperative for the ritual of exorcism to be performed. As pointed out before, it is the treatment of choice for demonic possession all round the world, and there is general agreement on its salient features. As we saw also in the African-type exorcism, it mobilizes the support of the social group, usually the extended family to which the patient belongs, by involving these people in the ritual. The Eurasian ritual, as we shall see, appears like the shortened version of the death and rebirth ceremony that the *vodun* priestess Lorgina used. However, it involves practically no physical handling of the patient at all, except for laying on of hands or touching with sacred objects. The exorcist appeals for help to the positive, "good" beings of the respective society's alternate reality. The evil possessing entities, which intially often refuse to make a personal appearance, are cited until they do. In other words, they are repeatedly forced to face both their victim and the exorcist. They are pushed into revealing their names and the reason they are plaguing the patient. They are then attacked by lengthy prayers and repeated cajoling, negotiations, and orders to leave. This is social drama on a grand scale, often also involving levity. Finally they admit defeat. They announce the day and the hour of their departure, and this pronouncement is strictly adhered to. It is like a contract that cannot be broken. The victim is delivered of the evil forces and is restored to health. In cases of severe or multiple possession, the exorcism may have to be repeated, for the demons fear and therefore resist being evicted, and once kicked out, they may return.

Although demonic possession cases are not seen very often, they are so spectacular that, for instance, in Europe and in the Near East, there are written records of them going back two thousand years. Perusing the stories of cases reported in the New Testament, in classical Greek sources, and in the Middle Ages, we find that, understandably, they do not give the entire picture as outlined above. But they do provide enough details so that they become instantly recognizable. Take the encounter between Jesus and a possessed man related by the Apostle Mark:

> They came to Gerasene territory on the other side of the lake. As he got out of the boat, he was immediately met by a man from the tombs who had an unclean spirit. The man had taken refuge among the tombs; he could no longer be restrained, even with a chain. In fact, he had frequently been secured with handcuffs and chains, but had pulled the chains apart and smashed the fetters. No one had proved strong enough to tame him. Uninterruptedly night and day, amid the tombs and on the hillsides, he screamed and gashed himself with stones. Catching sight of Jesus at a distance, he ran up and did him homage, shrieking in a loud voice, "Why meddle with me, Jesus, Son of God Most High? I implore you in God's name, do not torture me!" (Jesus had been saying to him, "Unclean spirit, come out of the man!") "What is your name?" Jesus asked him. "Legion is my name," he answered. "There are hundreds of us." He pleaded hard with Jesus not to drive them away from that neighborhood.
> It happened that a large herd of swine was feeding there on the slope of the mountain. "Send us into the swine," they begged him. "Let us enter them." He gave the word, and with it the unclean spirits came out and entered the swine. The herd of about two thousand went rushing down the bluff into the lake, where they began to drown. (V:1–13)

The ancient writer, in other words, notes the superhuman strength of the possessed man, his screaming, gnashing of teeth, and aggression against himself. The demon speaks from his mouth. The exorcism is stripped to its barest essentials: the demons identify themselves, beg not to be driven out, then name their conditions—they will leave, provided they may enter the swine. Then Jesus pronounces the exorcistic formula: "He gave the word." The exorcistic ritual is a complete success:

> The swineherds ran off and brought the news to field and village, and the people came to see what had happened. As they approached Jesus, they caught sight of the man who had been possessed by Legion sitting fully clothed and perfectly sane. (V:14–15)

As another example, a classical Greek writer of the third century, Flavius Philostratus, wrote a biography of a magician called Appolonius of Tyana. In it he tells of a woman seeking the help of the magician because her teenage son is possessed by a demon. The demon, she said, was dragging her son away to desolate places; he threatened to slay the boy; her son no longer had his own voice, uttering instead deep and rasping sounds like a grown man. In this case, we hear of the roaming of a possessed boy, his attempts at suicide, his changed, rough voice. Exorcism of the boy presupposes that demons will heed the written word. The demon had not allowed the woman to bring her son to the sage, threatening to kill him if she did. But the magician consoles her:

> "Be at peace," said the Sage; "he will not slay your child when he has read this." And he drew from his bossom a letter which he gave to this woman. The letter was addressed to the demon and contained the most terrible threats towards him.[4]

Presumably, the letter liberated the boy, for we hear nothing more about the matter.

From the Middle Ages, there is a description in the life story of the seventh-century saint St. Gall of a possessed girl who was brought to the monastery by her parents. As soon as she entered, the demon assaulted her, so that she fell to the floor. She began uttering "loud and terrible cries, accompanied by the most filthy words." She raged so furiously that several people tried in vain to hold her down.[5] The traits picked out there are an attack simulating epilepsy, coprolalia, and superhuman strength. A monk who took pity on her recited the exorcism over her, which freed her. He then explained to her what penances she should perform, including dietary restrictions. "But as the wretched woman made free use of forbidden meat the demon invaded her forthwith so strongly that she could hardly be held by several persons."

A relapse is a familiar occurrence, reported in many instances of demonic possession, although usually, unlike in the above case, no reason can be discovered. The exorcism appears to be successful, the demons are driven out, only to return with even greater fury. There is a detailed report of this frustrating problem from the 1830s in the works of Justinus Kerner, the German physician mentioned before.[6] This is not a sketchy tale like those quoted above, but an efficiently composed modern case history. Not only are the details fascinating, but the report gains added significance because Kerner was one of the therapists of the woman and an eyewitness to the major part of her demonic possession.

The case concerns a Lutheran peasant woman, Anna Maria Uz, born in 1799. She had always been healthy, was happily married, gave birth to three children, took good care of her family and her household, and was religious without being fanatical about it. In 1830, without any prior warning whatever, she was stricken by attacks of frightful convulsions. For four months she suffered from the most painful gnashing of her teeth during these seizures, and she kept thrashing about uncontrollably. Then suddenly one night in what seemed to be a condition of trance—in the parlance of his age (see chap. 2), Kerner called it "magnetic"—a demonic voice began speaking from her mouth. The alien being identified itself as the ghost of neighbor X, by recalling to Anna Maria's brother that when the latter was a boy, he had stolen sugarpears from him.

When Anna Maria came to, she recalled nothing of the exchange, and neither did she know that her brother had once stolen pears from this man. Subsequently, whenever this condition came upon her and X took over, her own individuality appeared to be totally extinguished. X would rage, curse in the vilest manner, especially venting his fury on God and everything sacred, and using her arms, he would viciously hit everyone around. That went on for a year; the woman's condition did not change even when she became pregnant again.

Since medication of various kinds did not help her, and apparently only prayer brought some relief, she was advised to go to the Catholic church in W., some distance from her village, and ask the priest there for an exorcism. On the way the demon raged terribly in her body, screaming and cursing. He threw her repeatedly up and down in the wagon by causing convulsions, so that those with her were afraid that she might go into labor. When they finally arrived in W., the priest refused to perform the exorcism, because Anna Maria was not a Catholic. But he did allow her to enter the church to pray there, which she did against violent protestations from the demon. For several hours she prayed in front of the altar in her own words, coming back once more the next day. That kept the demon away for eight weeks, so that she was able to have a normal delivery. But soon afterwards, he was back once more, torturing her even when during her lying-in she was nursing her infant, cursing and hitting her. Only when she had the newborn in her arms did he temporarily desist.

Renewed attempts at treating her medicinally remained unsuccessful. Dr. Kerner gives a list of the medications tried: ammoniate and a copper-sulfur compound, as well as herbal medicines all having a calming effect, such as valerian, deadly nightshade, asafetida, and thornapple. They had "no more effect than water." So she tried strenuous prayers again, once going to a particular chapel despite vicious opposition from her demon. After several hours in front of the altar, she fell backwards and lay for a long while as if dead. It was thought that this time she was definitely going to be liberated. But instead of one demon, after a few days two demons began speaking from her mouth and raging more than ever before, cursing and barking like dogs and screeching like cats.

Her family then took her to a peasant widely renowned for his magic and compassion. He treated her with prayers, laying on of hands, and communicating with the demons, whom he tried to talk into repenting and confessing their sins. After eleven weeks, the woman went through labor pains, and with an audible burst, one of her demons exited.

Unfortunately, the peasant could not continue with her treatment, for the authorities cited him for his healing activities, alleging that they were in violation of the law. He was later acquitted, but in the meantime, Anna Maria was taken home again, and the one demon still remaining in her once more started tormenting her. After fruitless efforts by still another physician, it was at this juncture, on 23 February 1833, that her husband brought her to Dr. Kerner's house:

> I soon came to know her as a decent, God-fearing woman who had been severely tested by her suffering. She appeared emaciated, and her eyes had a special ghostly, penetrating look. She constantly felt pain in them and maintained that it was through her eyes that the demons kept looking out.
>
> She easily tolerated my contention that it was not demons that caused her suffering, saying, "I don't care what people think it is, if only it could be stopped." Except for her attacks she showed absolutely no signs of any mental problem. Her attacks would start up without any physical cause and without premonition. She would suddenly shake all over and close her eyes, and at this moment the demon would start talking from her mouth. He identified himself as a miller from J., who had hanged himself fifteen years earlier. The woman had not known him and was quite young when he committed suicide. (p. 73)

During the attacks her pulse was low, and she would feel the demon only in her left side. In a by now familiar pattern, the demon spouted obscenities and insults against everything sacred. He would not allow her to eat properly, tolerating only a watery soup made from dark bread. He would cause Anna Maria to hit herself with her own fists, leaving her body black and blue. If she tried to pray, curses and fearful animal noises would issue from her lips instead; the demon would pull her tongue out of her mouth to incredible length and distort her facial muscles into a satanic grin. When she was free of attacks, she had severe headaches and suffered from intolerable pain in her abdomen, legs, and arms.

Kerner cites witnesses to a curious observation, namely, that the demon understood Latin (while the Lutheran peasant woman of course did not), correctly following such orders given in Latin as, "Lift your right arm," or "Shake your head." Herr von Wangenheim, a friend of Kerner's whom he had invited to observe Anna Maria with him, added another illustration of the extraordinary intellectual performances those possessed are capable of:

> She would kneel by the open window and in rapt devotion and with an imploring voice would speak the most beautiful prayers; she would with the deepest emotion and all from memory correctly recite the most lovely hymns, always those most proper for her situation. (p. 81)

As to treatment, Kerner tried infusions of St. John's wort, reputed to have antidemonic properties. But it produced furious rages. He used counseling and especially hypnosis, his specialty. He was quickly able to put her into a semidormant state, in which she would hear the voice of a protective spirit consoling her and promising speedy deliverance. But hypnosis could also call the demon into action, and it was obvious that he hated the kindly otherworldly helper. If Kerner then asked where the spirit of the woman was, he would say in a surly voice, "It went away with that scoundrel."

Occasionally, Kerner's efforts would bring what appeared to be relief. Anna Maria would step up to the window and with superhuman effort would vomit and blow, as if ridding herself of something. She would then fall backward in a faint and remain for fifteen minutes or so in a catatonialike condition. But the demon would come right back. Kerner came to the conclusion, also reached by modern therapists of multiples, that hypnosis was at most a useful adjunct; it could not cure the underlying problem. So Kerner decided to try another approach:

> When these continually alternating conditions had lasted for a long while, and both magnetism and medical treatment remained fruitless, I seemed to have no other choice but to return to the method of exorcism, which earlier had forced the supposed demons to relinquish their hold and seemed to provide at least some temporary relief to the afflicted woman. (p. 76)

Herr von Wangenheim tells how the exorcism with prayers and laying on of hands continued all day and well into the night:

> Toward one or two in the morning, the attacks seemed to lose some of their horror, and the language of the demon became milder, almost plaintive. He could feel, so he said through the mouth of the patient, that he would have to leave the body of the woman, but they should let him have some time and not pressure him so severely. . . . If they would realize how horrible it was outside (at this, the woman's body

shuddered), they would have pity on him and not beset him so cruelly. (p. 81)

Under hypnosis the following morning, Anna Maria reported that the demon was still in her, but that he was getting milder and that he was ready to repent. He would truly leave that day between eleven and twelve, but he could not do so before he confessed all his sins. They would have to write it all down, help him with questions, and continually remind him to tell the truth. That was done, and the emerging story was one of a man who during his lifetime had committed all manner of transgressions, drinking, fornication, lying, stealing, and adultery, and finally ended up a suicide. According to von Wangenheim, who recorded the confession, a number of details were later verifiid. Anna Maria had severe convulsions; she blew and screamed and three times fell into a dead faint. Then the demon was gone.

Unfortunately for the unhappy woman, her affliction started anew a few days later, this time with a different demon. It was expelled, but another one arrived, so that there had now been a total of five relapses. Deliverance finally came, but in a most unexpected manner for the reader, and Kerner's report ends on a engaging note of mystery.

> It had now become clear that merely driving out the demon did not suffice, because each time another would appear to take the place vacated by the preceding one. If the unfortunate woman was to be cured completely, a way had to be found to protect her in the future. Some friends of mine inquired for me and discovered that there was someone living far away who in addition to being strong in faith also had manifold experiences in these matters. I am not allowed to reveal anything more about him. He appeared and succeeded with the strength of his faith and his magic (which permits no closer description) in accomplishing what had not been possible before. He not only freed the unhappy woman of the demon but also protected her against any future possession. After a fierce three-day struggle and under the usual circumstances the demon left, a devil returning to the devils. (p. 91)

Anna Maria Uz never had any more demonic encounters, and more than a year later her husband wrote a happy letter to Dr. Kerner, saying that she continued well, praying and working and thanking God, who with the help of Dr. Kerner had freed her of the affliction that had burdened them all for so many years.

As to the mysterious healer in Kerner's account who so successfully prevented any further relapses in Anna Maria Uz, Kerner does not reveal his identity in either of his two books about demonic possession. The answer to the riddle was pieced together in painstaking archival research by the German folklorist Heino Gehrts, a well-known expert on Kerner's life and times,[7] and what he found only deepens the mystery. The name of the healer was Jacob Dürr. He was a tailor from Kirchheim unter Teck, a village near Tübingen, a university town in southern Germany. Gehrts calls him the last German shaman. This man was born in 1777. How he could possibly have had access to ancient and long-forgotten pagan traditions remains undiscoverable. But his contemporaries attest to the fact that he possessed what he called a magical belt, he had extensive knowledge of magical lore and formulas, and he knew how to make amulets and how to use them. He was an expert herbalist, composing innumerable highly effective potions and powders, as well as applying ancient fragrance therapy, by giving victims of demonic possession highly scented herbal sachets to smell in order to minimize demonic attacks. He was also clairvoyant, in continuous contact with the spirit world, communicating with its inhabitants in an "unintelligible spirit language." If he could not go immediately to the aid of a patient, he was known to send spirit helpers, and he told many amazing stories about the demons and the dead, the angels and the devils who were his daily associates.

Judging from accounts about him, Dürr must have been in a nearly continuous religious trance state, with his attendant disorientation being interpreted by his uncomprehending contemporaries as "drunkenness." But he was not a drunkard. As Professor Eschen-mayer, a friend of Kerner's, wrote, he had a peculiar constitution. Even a few drops of coffee would make him tremble, and a bit of wine put him into ecstasy. We are reminded of the ritual drinking of Central American shamans, who also use alcoholic beverages as a drug for trance induction. "What am I to do?" the sixty-year-old Dürr is reported as saying. "Where am I to get the strength for my cures? I am hardly able to eat anything, wine is the only thing that helps me replenish that strength."

Kerner appealed to Dürr for help when he realized that he could not successfully conclude the case of Anna Maria Uz, his first patient suffering from demonic possession. After working with Dürr, he understood that without his old peasant healer's exorcistic skills, he could not have accomplished her permanent cure. From then on, Kerner undertook no treatment for demonic possession without the help of the old shaman. When, some years later, Dürr overexerted himself during one such exorcism and seemingly lost his effectiveness, Kerner dissolved their partnership, sent home all the patients waiting for such treatment, and never again undertook any exorcism. Dürr, however, subsequently recovered his powers, and an astonishing number of successful cures performed by him are a matter of record.

That Kerner did not divulge Jacob Dürr's identity in his writings is not solely because of their parting of the ways. It was also an expression of the conflict between the new, scientifically grounded biomedicine propagated by the universities and folk health-care practices. This conflict, as Gehrts points out, was just beginning to emerge during the first decades of the nineteenth century. Academically trained physicians were struggling to wean people away from the barber, the smith, the clover master, and the herbalist, to whom they were used to turning for health care. The academicians had the state in their corner, and laws were passed against "quackery." Despite his obvious success as a healer, and against the pleas of his many patients, Dürr was repeatedly fined and even jailed. Kerner felt that the academic training he himself had received had robbed him of his naive but powerful faith, and it was for this reason that he was unsuccessful in healing demonic possession. Dürr was only one of a number of folk healers he turned to for help, although the most effective one, and by providing anonymity, perhaps Kerner was actually trying to protect his peasant shaman from further persecution.

Although nearly two centuries have passed, that conflict between folk tradition and the powerful establishment of modern medicine has not abated, as we shall see in the story of Anneliese Michel in the next chapter.

9 **T**WO RECENT CASES OF DEMONIC POSSESSION

Stories about possession by evil spirits have always fascinated people, and our own century is no exception. The film *The Exorcist,* based on an actual case, had numerous reruns both here and abroad. *Hostage to the Devil,* by the Jesuit father Malachi Martin,[1] which recreates six contemporary possession cases, was widely read in this country, and in the German-speaking parts of Europe, the case of a nurse called Magda, described by Adolf Rodewyk,[2] also a Jesuit father, has gone through four editions since it was first published in 1965.

Yet demonic possession is not just the stuff of scary stories. As explained before, we are dealing with actual, catastrophic physical and psychological changes, bringing great suffering to the afflicted. To demonstrate the point, I want in the following to describe two recent cases. They show first of all how little the symptoms of the affliction have changed over time, that is, how stable the syndrome actually is, and second, they raise the important question about what role, if any, modern psychiatry and allopathic medicine might play in the cure.

Both cases involve young girls. The one, called Marci, is from Xb., a small community of Maya peasants in Yucatán about six kilometers from Utzpak, the village where the Temple Congregation is located. The other one is Anneliese Michel, the German university student mentioned in the Introduction. In many ways, their possession experiences were identical, although they came from such vastly different backgrounds, the one from a traditional village, the other from a modern Western town. But there were also differences, as we shall see, the most significant being that Marci today is alive and well, and Anneliese died.

The Story of Marci.

Marci's possession experience and exorcism were related to me in January 1985, when I once again went to do some fieldwork with the Temple Congregation. The exorcism had been concluded a few weeks before I arrived, so it was the principal topic of conversation, all the more since Gregoria (not her real name), one of my most trusted coworkers, had been one of the two exorcists. Gregoria is a highly intelligent peasant woman, the mother of ten children and a dedicated member of the Temple Congregation. I interviewed Gregoria on tape and in addition spoke with everyone involved in the case, including Marci herself.

When Marci was twelve years old, her father, for a considerable sum of money, agreed with an old man to send the girl to him as a permanent sex partner. Earlier, he had successfully concluded a similar bargain involving his somewhat older stepdaughter. Marci, however, refused to go to the old man and stayed home. One day, when her mother had left for work in the family's cornfield, Marci's father prepared a dish of scrambled eggs and let Marci have some, too. Marci's mother later insisted that he had mixed a witching powder into Marci's portion. Such powders are sold openly on the market in Tizimin, a provincial town nearby. For soon after eating of those scrambled eggs, Marci became ill. She was disconsolate, she would cry incessantly, and for hours on end she restlessly ran up and down the Xb. village streets. Her mother took her to the physicians at the government clinic. After examining her, they came to the conclusion that she was suffering from *los nervios*. In Latin America, that is a catchall diagnosis whenever women complain of depression. No need to worry, it would pass, they said.

Instead, however, Marci's condition grew steadily worse. Her mother took her to "espiritistas," spiritualist healers in Tizimin and also in Motul, another provincial town. But Marci was frightened by the skulls she saw in those houses, and the healers could not help her. Marci hardly reacted any more when anyone tried to talk to her. She stripped before strangers, and once during a visit in Utzpak, she scandalized Gregoria's mother, Dona Eusebia, my principal field assistant, by going to the gate, pulling down her panties, and, pushing her pelvis forward, urinating while standing, in plain view of the men standing on the corner across the street. She also had numerous convulsive attacks. As Gregoria tells the story:

I saw Marci for the first time in the middle of 1983. I was on the market and I noticed her because her entire upper arm was burned. Since I did not know her, I asked a boy selling at a stall, "What happened to that girl?" "They say she fell into the hearth fire, into the food." "And why did she fall?" "They say she suffers from *los nervios*, and she also has attacks," he says.

The next day I saw her once more on the market, she was crouching in the middle of the street. "What is the matter with this girl?" I asked her mother. With a dispirited voice, her mother said, "She is sick. The doctors say it is *los nervios*. She just doesn't get any better. I have been taking her to the doctors for two years now, and they can do nothing for her." So I said to her, "If you believe that God can cure her, we have a temple here and you can go there and we will pray over her, so God will make her well." She just listened to me, but she never came to the temple, they say because she was a Catholic.

About half a year later on the market, I met Chucha, her mother's sister, who is a member of our congregation. She told me that Marci and her mother had come from Xb. to visit, but that Marci was very ill. So I said, "I'll come in the afternoon to see what is wrong with her, what the sickness is that she has, and we'll pray for her." I asked whether we should also tell Manuel, our preacher, to come. "No," she said, "we asked him, but he came only once and then did not come back. He said that she was possessed by demons, and he does not want to pray for her. He says that if a person such as he is not prepared, the demons will leave the girl and will possess him. Manuel is afraid of the Devil," says Chucha, "he can't resist him, that is why he doesn't come back." So I asked Brother Alfredo, he is also a preacher, and by way of his mother, he is related to Chucha.

Alfredo arrived at Chucha's house first and Marci was so sick that he left again to try to find somebody to help him with the prayer. "Come quickly," he said, "her mother is of no use to me, she has no idea what praying means, and she knows nothing of the Word of God." The girl, he said, was close to death. She was rolling on the floor, the Devil was about to kill her.

So we hurried to Chucha's house, he on his bicycle, I on foot, and we started to pray. As soon as we began, the Devil attacked her even worse. She writhed on the floor, foam came from her mouth, she had an attack, she could hardly stand it any more, she was close to suffocating and could no longer even scream. We continued to pray, and finally she quieted down and was able to get up from the floor. But she was not healed. She started to insult us in the most obscene way, even Alfredo, and she blasphemed God. Alfredo, who was not prepared for that, grabbed a piece of cane and started to beat her, but I demanded that he stop it. "We are fighting an evil spirit," I said, "and you are thrashing the flesh. It says in the Bible that the Devil can only be defeated with fasting and prayer."

During the following weeks, Gregoria and Alfredo, often joined by Gregoria's father and Chucha's son-in-law, came every day after the service in the temple and prayed for Marci for many hours. They tried to take her to the temple also, but Manuel forbade it, because she often had to vomit or spit, although her mother spread some paper on the floor in front of her. When she was awake, she would cry like a small child and begged them, "Let me die, I am burning up. They are torturing me, I am hurting all over, they want to kill me." Or she would say, "Don't pray, when you pray it burns me." Then she would start trembling and go into convulsions and writhe. Frequently Gregoria would have to hold her down while Alfredo read from the Bible, especially from the 91st Psalm, prayed in his own words, or laid the Bible on the raging girl. They tried to get her to kneel, but she resisted that. She often retched, as if she were about to vomit up something big. She would bring up quantities of foam, which left a bluish stain on the cement floor, and with that, her attack would stop, only to start over again. Even while she was lying in her hammock, foam would stream from her mouth and stand in puddles on the floor. At night sometimes those present would hear a noise as if a horse had jumped on the roof. The dishes clattered in the cupboard, and plaster fell from the walls. Then the demons announced themselves. Gregoria:

> We recognized the arrival of the Devil, because Marci would begin to curse, and she would urinate. That is why we knew that the Devil had come. Her urine had a terrible stench.

In the beginning, there were a large number of demons; later on only two remained, but they refused to give their names, although Gregoria kept asking for them. Marci had practically no schooling, she could neither read nor write, yet the demons sounded highly educated. They named a large number of places where "without using a bus or a plane" they had been roaming for the past two thousand years, localities in Mexico and in the United States and other places the names of which Gregoria did not recognize. The demons also described disputes in the temple, which Marci had no way of knowing about. When the demons spoke, they never sounded like Marci. They either used a thin, piping voice or the trembling voice of a very old woman, and even the deep one of an old man. There was a curious intonation to what they said, a monotonous singsong with an occasional choking glottal cutoff, which the eight-year-old daughter of Gregoria, who was often present at the prayers, delighted in imitating and demonstrating for me.

Even when there was no exorcistic prayer, Marci exuded a repulsive stench, so that her grandmother, who lived with the family in their one-room house, asked to be moved to relatives in the village, because she could not stand it. So the family constructed a hut of tarpaper and limestone for Marci and her mother some distance away from the house. That almost caused a tragedy. Marci's demons tried to kill the mother. Gregoria and a group of visiting women heard shouts, "Come on, help us, we'll kill her!" They arrived in the nick of time: Marci had her mother by the throat and was about to choke her to death.

She caused her family much anguish also in other ways. She kept attacking them with floods of insults and curses. She scandalized them by grabbing the cat and putting it to her breast as if nursing it. If she had an especially severe attack, even her grandmother began to tremble. Hideous creatures invaded the house, enormous tarantulas crawled through a crack in the wall and passed over the floor, and during the night, an owl kept screeching on the garden wall.

Marci also caught some of the chickens of her aunt, and even one of her precious turkeys. She killed them by twisting their necks and then tried to tear them apart with her teeth. She tore unripe, bitter bananas from the trees and ate them skins and all, and pulled hot chili peppers from the bushes and stuffed them whole into her mouth. She had enormous strength; she would uproot banana trees nine feet tall or more, or pick up large chunks of limestone, the building material of the area, and set them into the middle of the street. She also frequently threw stones at passersby, injuring at least one woman. With her hands as stiff as claws, she grabbed the tongue of her aunt and tore it. Chucha showed me the gash when I arrived in January. She always felt hot and kept begging her family to bathe her.

One day she escaped from her mother and got to a small chapel at the edge of the village, where a farmer had set up statues of the Virgin Mary and of San Isidro, the patron saint of peasants. She threw the statues out into the street, broke them, and then fled into the thorny bushes of an abandoned homestead. Her mother later found her and dragged her out by her hair. Had she stayed there over night, the enraged owner of the chapel would surely have slain her. At intervals, there were also times when she could not move at all, lying in her hammock as if dead.

The exorcistic prayers did not seem to do her much good. The rainy season had passed; the weather turned dry; it was October, then November. Repeatedly, Manuel said publicly in the temple that what the exorcists were doing was not of God. After all, the Apostles never had to pray for months when they exorcised evil spirits. They expelled them with a single command. It was obvious that the girl could not be cured. Even Marci's family was ready to give up. "I can't take it any

longer," her mother complained. "She rages day and night, she can't
sleep, not for a moment does she rest. She won't eat anything, she is
getting thinner and thinner. She is sure to die on us." The exorcists
finally agreed that they should seek medical help once more. Gregoria:

> So we went with her to the government clinic, Alfredo, myself,
> Chucha, and her mother. The doctor asked her, "When did your
> illness start?" Because we had told him what had happened. "I am not
> sick," she says. "For two thousand years I have been roaming this earth,
> for two thousand years I have been plaguing people in this way." "Your
> mother tells me that you are disrespectful to her, and that you scream a
> lot." "You never heard me do that, not a single time did you hear me
> like that," she answered. She talks completely sensibly. "Well," says the
> doctor, "there is no medicine for this kind of sickness. We can give you
> the money for the bus fare. I suggest you take her to Mérida to the
> insane asylum."
>
> We discussed the matter among ourselves, and I said, "We are not
> going to accept the money. After all, there is no way in which you can
> cure a spirit. All of you know that there are no cures for evil spirits.
> How could you possibly heal a spirit, it is like the wind. The physicians
> cannot see it, so how could they tell what is wrong with it? Even this
> physician, who is a Protestant, doesn't know the Bible well enough. He
> had no idea what Marci meant when she said, "I have been roaming
> this earth for two thousand years and am tormenting the people." This
> sort of thing, after all, didn't start here and now. You heard him ask the
> girl, "And why are you doing these things?" And the way she answered,
> "Why are you asking me these questions?"
>
> So Alfredo said, "All right, so let us leave. This physician cannot help
> us." "We are leaving now," he said to the doctor, "and we want to thank
> you," for the doctor had not asked us to pay for the consultation. He
> gave us a few pills, which we were supposed to give to Marci, so she
> would calm down a bit and could rest some. But after she took those,
> the demon raged even more furiously. I told her mother, "If you
> believe that your daughter will get well, then she will be cured, you just
> have to be patient, because we cannot know when God will work his
> miracles."

So the exorcists continued with their prayers, and occasionally, they
asked the demons when they would finally decide to leave. The usual
answer was, "We'll leave now, but tomorrow morning at five we will be
back." And punctually, as soon as the town-hall clock struck five, they
would return. But one day, about two weeks before Christmas, the
demon suddenly said, "In half an hour we'll leave, and we won't come
back." Gregoria:

> The next day, it was a Sunday, about eleven in the morning, exactly
> four weeks ago, I met Chucha on the market, and she said to me, "You

know what, Marci has been asleep since yesterday. She won't move, she won't get up, she doesn't wake up, she does nothing at all. She has not eaten any breakfast, either." "Let her be," I said, "I'll come as soon as I can." The family was afraid to wake her, because in the past, she had often struck them when they did that. About four in the afternoon, I went to Chucha's house. "She still didn't get up," her mother said. "She just lies there under her coverlet and doesn't move." I touched her, and she felt very hot. I tried to feel her pulse, but could not find it. I wondered whether she was having another attack. So I said to her mother, "Make a tea of crushed orange leaves." I try to lift Marci up, but can't do it. Tears come streaming from her eyes, but she cannot open them. I asked her if she hurt anywhere, but she shook her head. So I lifted her head a bit and gave her the decoction. She drinks half a cup full. So I say to her mother, "Make her something to eat." Then with the help of her brother, who is younger than I, we helped her to sit up in the hammock, for if we leave her lying there, she is going to die of hunger. She took the food and ate two whole cups full. "Better take it away from her now," I said to her mother. "She didn't eat anything yesterday, maybe she should have something again later." Then Marci got out of the hammock, went outside [to urinate], then came back and we started talking. "Why did you lie down yesterday?" I asked her. "I had a bellyache." "Will you come to the service at the temple tonight?" "Yes," she answered, quite normally.

They brought her a bucket of water, so she could take a bath, and in the evening, she came to the service. A different Brother conducted the service, not Manuel. We sang many hymns, and the Holy Spirit manifested itself in Marci, and she danced beautifully and it seemed that she was never going to stop.

During the first two weeks of January 1985, that is, a mere four weeks after her deliverance, I visited Marci and her family a number of times and spoke with her. She was shy, as teenage Maya girls usually are. Gregoria tried to get her to recount some of the things that the demons had said, but it was obvious that she had become completely amnesic with respect to the events of the past half-year. She did remember how her illness had started and she knew that she had been sick for a long time. Calmly she went about her work in the household and at the upright loom, where she and her mother were weaving hammocks for sale.

Gregoria worried privately whether the condition might not start again, because there was talk about the two women returning to Xb. She was afraid that Marci's father might once more try witchcraft against his daughter. Twice when Marci was so ill he had come to see her, but the oranges he brought had made the girl ill. There were also allegations that he sprinkled bewitching powder in Chucha's house, because after his visits, the demons always raged particularly furiously. So Chucha asked him not to come again. However, ac-

cording to letters I have received, Marci continues well. The last time I
saw Marci was at the temple the Sunday before I left Yucatán. She was
kneeling at the altar with her mother among those who had asked to
be baptized the following week.

If we compare what Marci experienced with the symptoms of demonic possession listed earlier, we note that the only item missing is
autoaggression, which is so prominent in the case of Anna Maria, as
described by Kerner. We might speculate that this extreme behavior
did not occur because the Apostolic exorcists got to their patient more
or less at the outset of the acute phase, which in the case of Kerner's
patient had recurred several times before Kerner was asked to treat
her.

The Story of Anneliese Michel.[3]

I was alerted to the case by a brief item in *Newsweek* (23 August
1976), which reported that this twenty-three-year-old university student, an epileptic, had died while being exorcized. Supposed demons,
among them Lucifer, Judas, Nero, and Hitler, had spoken from her
mouth. There were tapes available of the exorcistic sessions containing "incoherent screams mixed with furious profanity." I filed the
item for future reference as another modern case of demonic possession.

Unexpectedly, the affair had a sequel in the spring of 1978, when
an NBC television news program reported that Anneliese Michel's
case had occasioned a criminal investigation. At the ensuing trial, the
four defendants, Anneliese's parents and the two priests who with the
permission of their bishop had carried out the exorcism, were convicted of negligent homicide. They were sentenced to suspended jail
terms and court costs. It seemed from this turn of events that the
court was convinced of a causal connection between the exorcism and
the death of the girl. That was curious, because in all the many
religious communities worldwide where exorcism was practiced, the
experience was that the ritual *saved* the life of the afflicted, and *not*
doing it could lead to death. I decided to try and find out more about
the case.

Eventually, with the help of one of the defense lawyers, I was given
access to all of the court documents, more than eight hundred pages.
Father Renz, the principal exorcist, let me have a copy of the sound
tapes of forty-two exorcistic sessions. I went to Germany and interviewed all the principal characters involved in the story. Some of them
wrote down their own recollections for me. So short of actually being
there at the time of the exorcism, I had as complete a fieldwork record
as was possible to assemble after the fact. It made it possible for me to
reconstruct what happened to Anneliese Michel, and to formulate a
conjecture about why she died.

Anneliese was born in 1952, the daughter of a Catholic lower-middle-class artisans' family. Her father, and his father before him, owned a sawmill in Klingenberg, a small town in Bavaria, where Anneliese grew up. She was a sickly child and one year behind in school because of a number of childhood illnesses. But in her studies she did quite well. Then, about the time of her sixteenth birthday, she briefly blacked out in school, and the following night, she had a convulsive attack and bit her tongue. She felt that a giant force was pinning her down. It lasted about fifteen minutes.

An entire year went by uneventfully, then in August 1969 the same type of seizure occurred again. This time, her mother took her to the family physician, who referred them to Dr. L., a neurologist in Aschaffenburg, a larger town nearby. He ran a number of tests and found nothing wrong with her. As he told the court investigator later, "Neurologically and psychologically all findings were negative." The EEG was normal also. But in order to account for the two nocturnal seizures, he assumed that she probably had a cerebral disease of the convulsive type, that is, epilepsy. During the hearings, he was not sure whether he had prescribed the anticonvulsant Dilantin (phenytoin sodium) at this time, or whether that was later, at the second consultation.

With the start of the new school year, Anneliese became ill. She had to have her tonsils removed, then she contracted pleurisy and pneumonia, complicated by a tuberculous infection. By January, she had to be moved to a hospital in Aschaffenburg, and then to a sanatorium in the mountains of southern Bavaria. It was there, in June 1970, that another attack came. She was examined by a neurologist in the nearby town. Her EEG was normal, but since she had had attacks before, he recommended anticonvulsant medication. It was soon after this examination, while Anneliese was still in the sanatorium, that she had her first vision of cruelly grimacing demonic faces.

Although the frightening visions happened several more times, she did not tell the neurologist about them. Her EEG results were normal, and in August, she was discharged from the sanatorium. Just before the start of school in September, there was another seizure. Her new classmates found her withdrawn and "deeply religious." During checkups with various specialists, she was diagnosed as having some circulatory problems, but nothing was done about those. Instead the family physician, noting renewed seizures, prescribed another anticonvulsant.

The last two high-school years saw Anneliese increasingly apathetic and depressed. She had some episodes of brief "absences," that is, unconsciousness, then in June 1972, there was one last intense seizure, and after that the problem disappeared altogether. But remembering that an attack had occurred at the start of the previous school year, her worried mother insisted on another consultation with the Aschaffenburg neurologist. The EEG was normal and remained normal also during subsequent examinations, but in view of the history of seizures, he prescribed the anticonvulsant Dilantin.

Simultaneously, however, Anneliese felt anything but normal. She turned "stiff" more frequently, began smelling a horrible stench not noticed by others, the horrid grimacing faces beset her wherever she was, and an icy terror would well up in her body. Increasingly, she sought help in prayer, although her mother observed how when she passed by the statue of the Virgin Mary in the living room, her hands would turn to claws and her eyes would become jet black, as if she hated the Mother of God.

These problems became even more obvious when with her father she visited a shrine to the Virgin Mary in Italy, in San Damiano. The shrine was not accorded official recognition by Rome, but was very popular among the laity and was the goal for many organized pilgrimages. The visit turned into a shattering disappointment for Anneliese. She could not enter the shrine; the soil burned under her feet, and she had to avert her glance from a picture of Christ. On the way home in the bus, she ripped apart a rosary, she exuded a repulsive stench, and she spoke for the first time in a masculine, "unnatural" voice. She also mocked the pious tour guide and tore off a medal the woman was wearing. "My will was not my own," she was to say later. She felt that someone else was manipulating her, and she could do nothing about it.

Before going off to college in Würzburg in September of 1973, at her mother's insistence, she went back to Dr. L. for another examination. She complained that she had no power of decision and that she felt all empty inside. She told him of the ghastly distorted faces that were plaguing her and that she thought were inside her. She refused to describe what they looked like, but called them devils. When the physician asked what made her think that was what they were, she did not answer. She also predicted an imminent end to the world by fiery conflagration. He added another anticonvulsant to her medication, and, according to Anneliese's mother, he also suggested that they consult a Jesuit. It says something about the climate of the age that he later hotly denied this charge.

Anneliese never went back to him, seeking out specialists in Würzburg instead. And as an obvious reaction to Dr. L.'s skepticism, she never again mentioned the grimacing monsters or the end of the world to any representative of the medical profession. She told them only about what she apparently figured they could handle, her depression, her severe headaches, the continuing stench. For her other problems, those that she began to regard as exclusively within the confines of religion, she and her parents began consulting various priests.

The first one suggested medical attention. Recalling Dr. L.'s remark about a Jesuit, they next turned by mail to Father Adolf Rodewyk, the well-known author on demonic possession mentioned above. He thought possession was present, but declined to get involved because of his advanced age. He gave them the name of another priest, who also refused them, counseling neurological testing instead. But in the meantime, two young Aschaffenburg priests had heard of the case and had begun to take an interest in Anneliese's plight. One especially, Father Ernst Alt, although advising continued medical treatment, also began praying with her, and started writing to the bishop of the diocese on her behalf. He became increasingly convinced that an exorcism was needed, but official approval was necessary in the Catholic church before the ritual could be carried out, and the bishop hesitated. Such permission was granted only after an exhaustive examination of the case. So in the meantime Father Alt talked with her extensively, and that, together with his priestly prayers and blessing, did seem to ease her. She felt confident enough to move to Würzburg and begin college, majoring in elementary education.

Once there, however, and despite Father Alt's spiritual ministrations, her own lengthy prayers in Würzburg churches, and a sympathetic new boyfriend, Anneliese's problems got worse. At the University Neurological Clinic, an EEG showed some discharge in the left temporal region, which to the mind of the therapist in charge confirmed the diagnosis of epilepsy. Her medication was changed to Tegretol, but it brought no relief either. She was sent to group therapy sessions, where she felt entirely out of place. So she refused to continue with that. She suffered a sudden paralysis on the left side, but her EEG no longer showed any irregularities. Only prayers, Father Alt's counseling and blessings, and a few visits to San Damiano with her boyfriend, Peter, brought some help. But all in all, she felt that she was losing ground.

In the summer of 1975, Anneliese's maternal grandmother, who had lived with the Michel family, died, and on her weekly visits home, Anneliese also missed her two sisters, who had gone to work elsewhere. Only Roswita, her youngest sister, was still home. Her pervasive anxiety deepened; she began feeling that she was eternally damned. One of her friends at college recalled a scene at their dormitory from this time:

> I remember an incident from July 1975. I sat with her in her room, and her boyfriend Peter was also present. Suddenly, right in the middle of the conversation, her face contracted into a real *Fratze,* a hid-

eous, grimacing countenance that I cannot describe in detail. Her body became completely stiff. It took half an hour before the cramp disappeared. (1981:72)

Such attacks became more frequent. Anneliese took to her bed, unable to move or eat. Sometimes she would weep or scream uncontrollably. So finally, her parents took her home, and there, the acute phase broke out in full force. She walked around on legs as stiff as sticks. She tore up rosaries and raged in guttural screams. In a quiet interval, Peter took her to Würzburg so she could register for the next semester, but had to bring her back because of renewed attacks.

Now matters became even worse. Anneliese could not sleep, getting at most an hour's rest at night. Sometimes she would pray, but then continued shouting the same formula for many hours: "My Jesus, forgiveness and mercy, forgiveness and mercy. . . ." She rushed through the house up and down the steps, "bucking like a billy goat," in the words of Father Rodewyk, who had come to see her. She knelt down, then got up with incredible speed, until her knees became ulcerated, and still she continued. Then she would tremble and twitch, and would lapse into total rigidity for days.

She had superhuman strength, taking an apple, for instance, and, seemingly without any effort, squeezing it until the fragments exploded through the room. She grabbed Roswita and threw her to the floor like a rag doll. Her muscles tensed into hard cords, so she could not swallow and she started choking. Her body seethed with heat, and seeking relief, she rolled in the coal dust in the basement, filled an old iron kettle with icy water and jumped into that, or stuck her head into the commode in the bathroom. She tore her clothes off and ran around in the house naked. The bed was intolerable, so she tried sleeping in the cool attic, but then would scream all night and tear up and down the stairs. She stuffed flies and spiders into her mouth and chewed on coal, or on her urine-soaked panties. She attacked her parents with well-aimed blows and bit Peter in the arm.

Anything sacred in the house was fair game. She ripped the pictures of saints from the walls, tore apart rosaries, poured holy water from San Damiano down the drain, and shattered a crucifix. She reviled the priests who came to pray for her, saying to one, "Take your paws off me, they burn like fire." But from some unknown reaches, there also came consolation. Her dead grandmother and her sister who had died as a child appeared to her, and small wounds opened on her hands and feet in a shape that the family interpreted as the blessing of the stigmata.

In desperation, the family tried to get hold of Father Alt, but he was on vacation. So they turned to Father Rodewyk once more, who arrived at the beginning of September. In a letter to the state attorney, he described his encounter with Anneliese:

> When I entered the house, Anneliese Michel lay, fully dressed, on the floor of the kitchen and could obviously not be addressed. I am of the opinion that she was in a typical hypnotic state, in a kind of deep sleep.
>
> I should like to remark that such a state is a symptom of possession. I designate it as a crisis condition.
>
> First I went to the living room with her parents and had them report to me about the condition of their daughter. Then I directed them to bring Anneliese into the room and make her sit on the sofa.
>
> Her father led her in and held her by the hand because she tried to hit her parents. She did not look emaciated.
>
> I sat down beside her and held her hands. In her trance state a second personage announced itself, calling itself Judas. I had asked, "What is your name?" and the answer came, "Judas." She spoke with an altered, much lower voice.
>
> I had held her by her wrists. During the conversation I noticed that her cramped muscles relaxed. She came to and looked at me with surprise. Apparently it was not until then that she noticed me consciously. Subsequently I was able to carry on an entirely reasonable conversation with her. I told her that we would not desert her and that we would help her. I was thinking of priestly aid through exorcism.
>
> Suddenly the cramps started again. I asked her family to take her back to the kitchen. I told them that I knew enough about the case, that I had found confirmation of my surmise that we were dealing with a case of possession, and that I would have to consider what could be done. When I left the house, Anneliese came out of the kitchen and slapped my cheek. (1981:85)

After returning to his home in Frankfurt, Father Rodewyk formulated an opinion, arguing that Anneliese was indeed possessed, and emphasizing in particular that she exhibited a loathing of sacred objects and a fear of exorcism, and that the demon that had taken over her body had betrayed his identity. As a result of Father Rodewyk's influence and of some additional correspondence with Father Alt, the bishop finally gave his official consent for an exorcism to be carried out and appointed Father Arnold Renz, a parish priest from a locality near Klingenberg, to carry out the ritual.

The great exorcism of the Roman Catholic church was committed to writing last in the *Rituale Romanum* in the seventeenth century. It is traditionally recited in Latin. Since it is not a sacrament but a rite, the exorcist has considerable latitude in varying what he says and in which language, and Father Renz made extensive use of this, which gave the exorcisms on the tapes great immediacy and power.

As generally done in exorcistic rituals, the Roman Catholic exorcism provides for those present to be the person possessed, the exorcist, and a community, most often family and friends of the afflicted person. The rite starts out with an invocation, spoken communally, to God and all the angels and saints. It continues with other prayers and Bible passages, interspersed with many Lord's Prayers and Hail Marys. The exorcist may sprinkle holy water and touch the possessed person with a sacred object, his stole, a crucifix, or some relic. At irregular intervals, he directs his questions at the possessing demon. Why did he possess the sufferer? When did he intend to leave? What was his name? There follow the exorcistic commands: the demon, once named, is ordered to leave his victim and return to hell whence he came.

Anneliese's first exorcism took place on 24 September 1975. For that session, we have no tape, only Father Renz's diary entry. It affords us a good impression of how quickly Anneliese learned to enter the trance, that is, to institute ritual control over the possession:

> 24 September 1975. Arrive at 16 hours. Started exorcism according to instructions. Anneliese, or rather the demons, behaved rather quietly at first. Anneliese is being shaken more and more strongly. Anneliese, or rather the demons, react most violently against the holy water. She starts screaming and raging.
>
> Anneliese knows everything. She knows what it is that she said; apparently she is always fully conscious. No amnesia at all. Anneliese is held by three men [so she would not injure herself or others], by Herr Hein, her friend Peter, and her father. She wants to bite right and left. She kicks toward me. Sometimes she simply hits toward the front. At first she sits on a chair, then on the couch. She is not allowed to remain lying down. Sometimes she does it but has to get up again right away. She complains that the devil sits in her lower back.
>
> Occasionally she screams, especially if she is sprinkled with holy water. At times she howls like a dog. Repeatedly she says, "Stop with that shit," or "You shit guy," "You dirty sow," "Put away that shit" (holy water). Actually she does not say very much, uses even the obscenities sparingly.
>
> In the end, during the Gloria Patri which we pray together repeatedly, she becomes furious. The entire session lasted from 16 hours to 21:30.
>
> Afterwards she said, "You should have continued." Apparently she felt that the demons were being routed. When she said good-bye she was actually quite lively. The entire matter must be very strenuous for her. She consumes a lot of energy, considering that three men are holding her down, and she continually struggles against them. (1981:95–96)

During the following weeks, a total of six demons announced their presence and stubbornly refused to be expelled, growling and cursing in their gravelly voices. Because they had so many fascinating things to say, especially about the reforms introduced as a result of the decisions of the Second Vatican Council, Father Renz soon decided to tape the sessions. Father Alt also came frequently from Ettleben, his new parish, to participate in the rite. Anneliese felt well, continued with her studies in Würzburg, and came home to Klingenberg every few days for exorcistic sessions. She also conscientiously took her Tegretol medication.

Around the middle of October, kindly beings began approaching her, especially the Virgin Mary, but also the Savior, and she started a diary of these revelations, which she wrote down as she was hearing them; or, rather, as she put it, "I don't hear voices exactly, I am given to understand" (1981:116). Simultaneously, the demons appeared to be weakening. Finally, on 31 October, a date repeatedly predicted both in her revelations and by the demons, the evil spirits were expelled one by one. In each instance the exit took place with Anneliese straining enormously, retching and vomiting. Unfortunately, as the small community around her was giving thanks in prayer and song, a new, unnamed demon announced its presence.

From then on, things went steadily downhill. The exorcistic sessions were continued, but the new demon was more and more taciturn, and by February fell silent altogether, as did his heavenly counterpart. Anneliese could no longer eat, battered herself bloody, and went into unceasing convulsions and screaming fits, while in lucid intervals steadfastly refusing to seek any more medical help. She died on 1 July 1976, on the day when she had predicted that "all will be well."

Quite clearly, what the three women, Anna Maria a century and a half ago, Anneliese in the 1970s, and Marci in the 1980s, suffered through was a nearly identical process. In all three instances, their symptoms agreed almost in every point with the list given in chapter 6. For Marci, there was no positive being giving her help. But then, perhaps she did not bother to tell about it, or it was not reported. Also, her exorcists were alerted to her plight and started the exorcism at the onset of the acute phase. That may have made matters easier, and a relapse, which both Anna Maria and Anneliese suffered, became less likely for the same reason. Anneliese, however, was the only one to be aware of what the demons were saying from her mouth and to remember much of it. As she used to say, she found herself confined in a hole, and from there, she was able to perceive what was going on. That is quite unusual and may well have come about because of her lengthy battle trying to convince the church authorities that she needed their help, so that she had to have a very clear idea of what was going on. In a way, possibly, she trained herself to re-member.

The question is, why did she die? The court assumed that she was killed by the exorcism, in the sense that she should have had medical attention instead. As one of the psychiatrists consulted as an expert by the court suggested, she should have been tranquilized, force-fed, and treated with electroshock. The psychiatrists, however, as is clear from their depositions, knew absolutely nothing about demonic pos-session and exorcism. Neither were they aware of the multiple person-ality experience, where a treatment such as suggested above does not work either.

In retrospect, it would be difficult even for a physician to decide what exactly killed her. The autopsy report blames starvation. We could speculate, however, that the psychoactive medication she was given, much more powerful than anything Dr. Kerner tried on Anna Maria, may in fact have prevented just those brain processes that needed to take place in order to free her of her affliction. There is some evidence for this view on the tapes. When the demons speak, their utterances show the typical glossolalia curve, as I was able to determine in the phonetic laboratory by analyzing the soundtrack. In her last phase, however, shortly before she died, Anneliese's screams no longer had this typical intonation pattern. Father Renz intuitively noted the same thing. "The demon has nothing to say," he says repeatedly on the last tape. The "window on brain processes," as I called the glossolalia pattern earlier (see chap. 1), showed instead a straight, undifferentiated line: she had lost the ability to go into trance, surely a most terrible thing to happen under the circum-stances.

ONCLUSION

How About Demons—and Other Spirits?

In this concluding chapter, we now need to come to grips with two conflicting ideas about human nature, as was outlined in chapter 1. We referred to the matter there as the theory of humans as bio-psychological systems as against the "soul theory." After coming to know so many different instances of possession, involving benevolent, dangerous, and evil beings or entities, it is logical that we should now want to consider the question, how real are they? Is the American anthropologist Weston La Barre right when he quips, "Nothing down here but us people"? And does it even matter? In this discussion, I want to contend that there are good reasons why we need to take a second look at positions such as the one taken by La Barre, and that it indeed matters; it matters a great deal.

If we maintain that in our world, people are real and spirits are not, that is in the final analysis merely an opinion. It presupposes that we know what we mean by "real." In the Western world, the debate about the nature of reality has raged ever since the Greeks first put stylus to clay tablet. Every time there was a significant change in cultural circumstance, the idea about what reality was shifted accordingly, and reality itself seemed to become less and less knowable. Finally Newton came to the conclusion that while the vibrations of sounds and colors struck the media of the senses, and this was transmitted to the mind, the real world was hidden behind these phenomena. The attributes we were sure we perceived were only our contribution. Modern natural science, after a period of extreme hubris when it was sure that its new instruments were capable of discovering "objective" reality, has come back to this stance. It admits that it is not possible to separate the observer from what is being observed. An anthropologist would take this opinion one step further by saying that what is accepted as being real in a particular situation is decided not by the individual but by the culture into which the situation is embedded.

This culturally relative rather than absolute nature of reality causes no problems as long as humans are part of a small, homogeneous, and, most important, egalitarian society: Everyone agrees more or less on what is real and what is not. However, increasingly in this century, humans are finding themselves in huge, complex state organizations. These societal structures are not egalitarian. There are those that have power and prestige and those that do not. What is real, then, is actually dictated by the convictions of the powerful, the prestigious in such stratified societies.

As could be expected, not everyone in a large, Western-type society has the same idea about what reality is. There will be those at the forefront of research and thinking who have the most recent tolerant attitudes of the subjective, relative nature of reality. They are the secure ones, the least likely to decree that others are wrong if they hold different convictions. But they represent the vanguard, and they are not all that numerous. To the far greater proportion of the prestigious and powerful, that is still news, and they are not willing to give up the view of the world that awarded them both security and power. They have learned a lot about the laws of nature, and they know definitely, unshakably what reality is, and it does not include spirits. Nothing down here but us people.

What happens to religion under such circumstances? If the faiths in question are merely that, namely, faiths, convictions, theology, thought systems, they will create accommodations, as the Second Ecumenical Council attempted to do for Roman Catholicism. But accommodation does not work when the respective religious style includes experience, as it does in possession. Experience is the most powerful of all persuaders. So instead of compromise, there is conflict.

In our sample, the conflict was least strident in those societies where there was still a safe bedrock of experiential tradition. Figge tells the following story from Rio de Janeiro:

> As I was walking along a dark, dead-end passage in the bush, far from any kind of dwelling, two men blocked my way. A third had withdrawn previously, but these two doubtless wanted to attack me. With courage born of desperation, I walked toward them with an energetic step, looked them straight in the eye, and greeted them with a loud "Boa noite!" "Good night." I assumed that their obvious confusion and my subsequent escape were the result of my courageous behavior, which they had not expected. I was disabused later when both in Umbanda centers and also outside, I came to know persons pos-

sessed by *exu* spirits who were in the habit of walking up to strangers, staring at them, and greeting them with "Boa noite!" (1973:51)

The currency of manifold native traditions in Brazil, not only Umbanda but also Candomble and others, prevents situations where someone participating in or accidentally straying into a possession experience would end up in a neurological clinic. The situation is similar in Japan. For others, their experience may result in severe and potentially destructive culture conflict. They are driven simultaneously to respect the view of the prestigious authority figures, and yet to cling to the powerful impulses generated by their experiences. For some, that may result in totally unsettling their inner adjustment. An illustration comes from the history of Spiritualism. Serious disagreements arose between the three Fox sisters, according to some because of the influence of some Catholic clergymen, but we cannot underestimate the powerful influence of the "scientific," that is, antispiritualistic, bent of the age. Margaret Fox sought refuge in alcoholism and publicly recanted in 1888, denouncing her experiences and abilities. She thought better of it later, but the incident shows the severe pressures under which she and her sisters must have suffered in that particular cultural situation.

The attacks directed at the Pentecostals are well known, usually taking the form of allegations that the speaking in tongues is faked. But the worst situation in the West is the one involving demonic possession. Those afflicted by it need help. Exorcism works, other strategies do not, yet their diagnosis and treatment are determined not by what works but by the prevailing attitudes, the paradigm concerning the nature of reality.

I recall a somewhat unsettling incident at the University of Freiburg a few years ago, shortly after my book about the Anneliese Michel case had come out in German. I met a lawyer turned Protestant theologian who had just received a professorship in religion at the university. He had some kind words about the book, but then went into a furious tirade, reviling Anneliese's home environment that fostered "such superstition" and literally raging against the priests who in this modern day and age would not know any better and see to it that she was taken to an asylum for treatment. Despite the fact that according to public opinion polls conducted in 1983, only fourteen percent of the Germans questioned believed in hell, as against sixty-six percent in the United States, and a mere eight percent thought the devil was real as against the same sixty-six percent in this country, this man clearly felt profoundly threatened. The same attitudes were reflected in a number of reviews that came out on the same book in the German-language press. The position is so ingrained that arguments that religious experience is accompanied by measurable and recordable physiological changes are totally ignored. In a 1984 article about the Anneliese Michel case, written by a physician and by a psychologist and published by a German parapsychology journal,[1] the argument that the ritual of exorcism induced the religious trance in Anneliese as proved by a laboratory analysis, and that this gave her control over her affliction, was totally disregarded, although the authors had at their disposal a complete set of all the exorcistic tapes. Neither of the two men bothered to check this argument on their own, contending instead that the existence of a religious trance was mythology and that such phenomena as were supposedly exhibited by Anneliese could also be encountered in other psychotic states. Ruling paradigms have a way of creating blind spots of this nature.

In the end, what can we say about the reality of spiritual beings? We can at least point out that the experience of their presence during possession is accompanied by observable physical changes. We should remember that whether these changes are internally generated or created by external agencies is not discoverable. No one can either prove or disprove that the obvious changes of the brain map in possession or in a patient with a multiple personality disorder, for that matter, are produced by psychological processes or by an invading alien being. Beyond that, as cultural anthropologists, we can call attention to the fact that the characteristics of these beings change in the course of cultural evolution, so they are part of the very real cultural scene. We can also point out that in all religious communities around the world, of whatever cultural allegiance, people indicate by their behavior that for them, spirit beings are part of the larger, all-encompassing reality. As contact with such experiences in an ever-shrinking world becomes more frequent, it behooves us to treat what others experience with respect, and should we encounter the believers as suffering human beings, to confront them on their terms and not on our own.

NOTES

Preface

1. Felicitas D. Goodman, *The Exorcism of Anneliese Michel* (New York: Doubleday, 1981).

1. Possession's Many Faces

1. The social scientists mentioned in this chapter are variously called ethnographers, folklorists, and anthropologists. An ethnographer is a specialist who describes a particular group of people. Both anthropologists and folklorists work as ethnographers in this sense. Traditionally, folklorists were specialists working within their own complex societies, while anthropologists concentrated on small, non-Western societies alien to their own. But in the course of this century, the two disciplines borrowed many interests and approaches from each other, and the distinction between them has become blurred. In our discussion, we are retaining the difference in terminology simply because this is how the respective researchers identify themselves.

2. Napoleon A. Chagnon, *Yąnomamö: The Fierce People,* 2d ed. (New York: Holt, Rinehart and Winston, 1977).

3. Felicitas D. Goodman, *Speaking in Tongues: A Cross-Cultural Study of Glossolalia* (Chicago: University of Chicago Press, 1972).

4. Vilmos Diószegi, *A sámánhit emlékei a magyar népi müveltségben* (Budapest: Akadémiai Kiadó, 1958) ("Traces of Shamanism in Hungarian Folk Culture," translation by me).

5. Erika Bourguignon, *Religion, Altered States of Consciousness, and Social Change,* Introduction (Columbus: Ohio State University Press, 1973).

6. My thanks to my colleagues George Apple, Dale Fitzgerald, and Minoru Tanaka for their tapes.

7. Charles M. Fair, *The Physical Foundations of the Psyche* (Middletown, Conn.: Wesleyan University Press, 1963).

8. Barbara W. Lex, The Neurobiology of Ritual Trance, in *The Spectrum of Ritual: A Biogenetic Structural Analysis,* ed. Eugene d'Aquili (New York: Columbia University Press, 1979), pp. 117–51.

9. Ingrid Müller, dissertation (in progress); supervision of the experiments by Professor Johann Kugler, M.D., Chairman of the Department of Psychiatric Neurophysiology of the Psychiatric Clinic and Policlinic of the University of Munich.

10. Felicitas D. Goodman, Body Posture and the Religious Altered State of Consciousness: An Experimental Investigation, *Journal of Humanistic Psychology* 26(1986):81–118.

11. Miles E. Drake, M.D., Department of Psychiatry, Ohio State University.

12. Mircea Eliade, *Shamanism: Archaic Techniques of Ecstasy* (Princeton: Princeton University Press, 1964).

13. Melville J. Herskovits, *Life in a Haitian Valley* (Garden City, N.Y.: Doubleday, 1971).

14. Erika Bourguignon, *Possession* (San Francisco: Chandler and Sharp, 1976).

15. The topic is treated, for instance, by Ralph B. Allison, The Possession Syndrome on Trial, *American Journal of Forensic Psychiatry* 6(1985):46–56; M. G. Kenny, Multiple Personality and Spirit Possession, *Psychiatry* 44(1981):337–58; Traugott K. Oesterreich, *Possession and Exorcism* (New York: Causeway Books, 1974); L. Rice, Disintegrated Personalities—or Possession? *Journal of the American Society for Psychical Research* 32(1938):69–80; and V. K. Varma, M. Bouri, and N. N. Wig, Multiple Personality in India: Comparison with Hysterical Possession State, *American Journal of Psychotherapy* 35(1981):113–20.

16. Corbett H. Thigpen and Hervey M. Cleckley, *The Three Faces of Eve* (New York: McGraw-Hill, 1957).

17. W. Herbert, The Three Brains of Eve, *Science News* 121 (1982):356.

18. I am grateful to Drs. Putnam, Pitblado, and Caul for answering my many questions.

19. Kaja Finkler, *Spiritualist Healers in Mexico* (South Hadley, Mass.: Bergin and Garvey, 1985).

20. Felicitas D. Goodman, Possible Physiological Mechanisms Accounting for Some Cases of Faith Healing, *Medikon* 3, nos. 6/7(1974):39–41.

21. In her chapter 9, "How Spiritualist Healers Heal," Kaja Finkler (n. 9) gives a useful summary of present thinking on the differences between Western biomedical treatment and faith healing; she substantially agrees with the position expressed in my article under n. 20.

22. Bernard Grad, Some Biological Effects of the "Laying on of Hands." A Review of Experiments with Animals and Plants, *Journal of Parapsychology* 29 (1965):95–129.

23. M. J. Smith, Paranormal Effects on Enzyme Activity, *Human Dimensions* 1, no. 2 (1972):15–19.

2. Spiritualism

1. For further details, see Felicitas D. Goodman, *Ecstasy, Ritual, and Alternate Reality: Religion in a Pluralistic World* (Bloomington: Indiana University Press, forthcoming).

2. Wolf-Dieter Storl, *Shamanism among Americans of European Origin* (diss., University of Bern, Switzerland, 1974); idem, Die Indianer der Spiritisten, *Wiener Ethnohistorische Blätter* 26(1983):3–18.

3. The terms *cult, sect,* and *religion* will be used interchangeably, referring more to the size of a group than to possible relative merit.

4. Quoted from Arthur C. Doyle, *The History of Spiritualism* (New York: George A. Doran, 1926).

5. Irving I. Zaretsky, In the Beginning Was the Word: The Relationship of Language to Social Organization in Spiritualist Churches, in *Religious Move-*

ments in Contemporary America, ed. Irving I. Zaretsky and Mark P. Leone (Princeton: Princeton University Press, 1974), pp. 116–213.

6. George Lawton, *The Drama of Life after Death: A Study of Spiritualist Religion* (New York: Henry Holt, 1932).

7. Whitney R. Cross, *The Burned-Over District: The Social and Intellectual History of Enthusiastic Religion in Western New York* (New York: Cornell University Press, 1950).

8. Peter Worsley, *The Trumpet Shall Sound* (New York: Schocken, 1968).

9. Raymond R. Moody, *Life after Death* (Bantam Books, 1975).

10. Leslie A. Fiedler. *The Return of the Vanishing American* (New York: Stein and Day, 1968).

11. Quoted in Lawton 1932, 337.

12. Kaja Finkler, *Spiritualist Healers in Mexico: Successes and Failures of Alternative Therapeutics* (South Hadley, Mass.: Bergin and Garvey, 1985).

3. Healing in Umbanda

1. Esther Pressel, Umbanda Trance and Possession in São Paulo, Brazil, in *Trance, Healing, and Hallucination: Three Field Studies in Religious Experience,* by Felicitas D. Goodman, Jeannette H. Henney, and Esther Pressel (New York: Wiley Interscience, 1974), pp. 113–226.

2. Horst F. Figge, *Geisterkult, Besessenheit und Magie in der Umbanda-Religion in Brasilien* (Freiburg: Alber, 1973); translation of the sections quoted by me.

4. Pentecostalism: A New Force in Christendom

1. John Thomas Nichol, *The Pentecostals* (New York: Harper and Row, 1971).

2. In the 1960s, a tract was distributed to the congregations of the Streams of Power movement, telling the following: "Some years ago Tommy Hicks was in Russia. Suddenly his interpreter left him. . . . Then he began to speak in tongues and the Holy Spirit gave him the language of those to whom he was speaking."

3. Details in Felicitas D. Goodman, *Speaking in Tongues: A Cross-Cultural Study of Glossolalia* (Chicago: University of Chicago Press, 1972).

4. Felicitas D. Goodman, Disturbances in the Apostolic Church: A Trance-Based Upheaval in Yucatán, in *Trance, Healing, and Hallucination: Three Field Studies in Religious Experience,* by Felicitas D. Goodman, Jeannette H. Henney, and Esther Pressel (New York: Wiley Interscience, 1974), pp. 227–364.

5. From a document entitled "Spirit, Order, and Organization," approved by the Faith and Order Commission of the World Council of Churches in August 1971. Quoted in Cyril G. Williams, *Tongues of the Spirit* (Cardiff: University of Wales Press,1981), p. 95.

6. The articles collected in David Martin and Peter Mullen, eds., *Strange Gifts* (Oxford: Basil Blackwell, 1984), illustrate the waning of the traditional Pentecostal and Charismatic movements in England, while another innovation, the "Restoration" House Churches, clearly geared toward ecstasy, is beginning to gain ground.

5. The Dangerous Spirits of Japan

1. I did fieldwork in Japan in 1975 and returned once more in 1982.
2. James W. White, *The Sōkagakkai and Mass Society* (Stanford, Calif.: Stanford University Press, 1970).
3. Harry Thomsen, *The New Religions of Japan* (Rutland, Vt.: Charles E. Tuttle, 1963).
4. For details concerning the folk beliefs about fox spirits, see Carmen Blacker, *The Catalpa Bow: A Study of Shamanistic Practices in Japan* (London: George Allen and Unwin, 1975), pp. 51–55.
5. Blacker, pp. 202–207, gives details of Deguchi's spirit journey.
6. Winston Davis, *Dojo: Magic and Exorcism in Modern Japan* (Stanford, Calif.: Stanford University Press, 1980).
7. Some authors, Winston Davis (see n. 6), for instance, consider this concern with unhappy spirits who need to be exorcized so they will no longer cause any harm to their families to be an indication of the influence of Western Spiritualist thought. The similarity may be an accidental convergence of traits, however, for Japan shares this tradition with all horticulturalist societies, few if any of which ever had any contact with modern Spiritualism.
8. Blacker, pp. 252–53.

6. The Multiple Personality Experience and Demonic Possession

1. Legendlike folk narratives shared by PSI enthusiasts include multiple personality accounts, however. An interesting article about this topic was published by W. K. McNeil, Mrs. F.-Little Joe: The Multiple Personality Experience and the Folklorist, *Indiana Folklore* 4, no. 2 (1971):216–45.
2. F. W. Putnam, Jr., R. M. Post, J. J. Guroff et al., One Hundred Cases of Multiple Personality Disorder (Paper presented to the Annual Meeting of the American Psychiatric Association, New Research Abstract #77, New York, 30 April–6 May 1983).
3. Frank W. Putnam, Jr., Dissociation as a Response to Extreme Trauma, in *Childhood Antecedents of Multiple Personality,* ed. R. P. Klupf (Washington, D.C.: APA Press, 1985), pp. 66–97; p. 77.
4. Putnam 1985, p. 71.
5. This benevolent helper and its role were first identified by Ralph B. Allison. See his book, written with Ted Schwarz, *Minds in Many Pieces* (New York: Rawson, Wade, 1980), chap. 5.
6. Edward W. Beal, Use of the Extended Family in the Treatment of Multiple Personality, *American Journal of Psychiatry* 135 (1978):539–42.
7. Jeffrey M. Brendsma and Arnold M. Ludwig, A Case of Multiple Personality: Diagnosis and Therapy, *International Journal of Clinical and Experimental Hypnosis* 22(1974):216–33.
8. Quoted in Frank W. Putnam, Jr., The Psychophysiological Investigation of Multiple Personality Disorder: A Review, *Psychiatric Clinics of North America* 7(1983):31–39; p. 31.
9. As we know from E. Lancaster, *The Final Face of Eve* (New York: McGraw-Hill, 1958), the original Eve White's autobiography.
10. Milton Rosenbaum and Glenn M. Weaver, Dissociated State: Status of a Case after 38 Years, *Journal of Nervous and Mental Disease* 168(1980):597–603.

11. Louise Rice, Disintegrated Personalities?—Or Possession? *Journal of the Society of Psychical Research* 32(1938):69–80; this is not the same incident also known as the Valentine's Day Massacre, where in 1977 five brothers were victims of a Manson-type slaying in Hollandsburg, Indiana.

12. See Allison (n. 4), chaps. 3 and 8.

13. Ralph B. Allison, The Possession Syndrome: Myth, Magic, and Multiplicity (Paper presented to the Second Pacific Congress of Psychiatry, Manila, Philippines, 12–16 May 1980); the incident is also mentioned in his book (n. 4), p. 199.

7. The Ghosts That Kill

1. Adolf Rodewyk, *Possessed by Satan,* trans. Martin Ebon (New York: Doubleday, 1975); originally published in German as *Dämonische Besessenheit* (Aschaffenburg: Patloch, 1963).

2. P. M. Schwarz, *Teufel, Dämone, Besessene: Das Reich der Finsternis* (Wien: Kreuz Verlag, 1976).

3. Alfred Métraux, *Voodoo in Haiti* (London: André Deutsch, 1959).

4. Felicitas D. Goodman, *Ecstasy, Ritual, and Alternate Reality: Religion in a Pluralistic World* (Bloomington: Indiana University Press, forthcoming), chap. 4.

5. Stephen D. Glazier, Pentecostalism, Exorcism, and Modernization (Paper presented to the Annual Meeting of the American Anthropological Association, Houston, Texas, 1977).

8. A Legion of Demons

1. No worldwide catechism has been issued by the Catholic church. The quotation is taken from the one just published in West Germany: *Katholischer Erwachsenen Katechismus: Das Glaubensbekenntnis der Kirche* (Bonn: Deutsche Bischofskonferenz, Verband der Diözesen Deutschlands, 1985).

2. Quoted in Traugott K. Oesterreich, *Possession and Exorcism,* trans. D. Ibberson (New York: Causeway, 1974), p. 13.

3. Alois Döring, Dämonen geben Zeugnis: Teufelsglaube und Exorzismus in traditionalistischen Bewegungen, *Schweizer Archiv für Volkskunde* 81(1985):1–23.

4. Oesterreich (n. 2), pp. 10–11.

5. Oesterreich (n. 2), p. 12.

6. Justinus Kerner, Geschichten Besessener neuerer Zeit, in *Sämtliche Werke,* ed. Walter Heichen, pp. 69–92 (translation by me); I am grateful to Dr. Heino Gehrts for providing me with the German original of this and the following report.

7. Heino Gehrts, Jacob Dürr aus Kirchheim, der letzte deutsche Schamane, in *Der Teckbote,* 16 June 1962; idem, Der Schneider von Kirchheim, in *Der Teckbote,* 16 November 1963 (translation by me).

9. Two Recent Cases of Demonic Possession

1. Malachi Martin, *Hostage to the Devil: The Possession and Exorcism of Five Living Americans* (New York: Reader's Digest Press, 1976).

2. Adolf Rodewyk, *Dämonische Besessenheit heute: Tatsachen und Deutungen,* 4th ed. (Stein am Rhein: Christiana, 1976).

3. Felicitas D. Goodman, *The Exorcism of Anneliese Michel* (New York: Doubleday, 1981).

Conclusion

1. Johannes Mischo and Ulrich J. Niemann, Die Besessenheit der Anneliese Michel, *Zeitschrift für Parapsychologie und Grenzgebiete der Psychologie* 25 (1983):129–93.

BIBLIOGRAPHY

Akhbar, Salman, and Byrne, Jessica Price. 1983. The Concept of Splitting and Its Clinical Relevance. *American Journal of Psychiatry* 140:1013–16.

Allison, Ralph B. 1980. *Minds in Many Pieces*. New York: Rawson, Wade.

———. 1980. The Possession Syndrome: Myth, Magic, and Multiplicity. Paper presented to the Second Pacific Conference of Psychiatry, Manila, Philippines, 12–16 May.

———. 1985. The Possession Syndrome on Trial. *American Journal of Forensic Psychiatry* 6:46–56.

Beal, Edward W. 1978. Use of the Extended Family in the Treatment of Multiple Personality. *American Journal of Psychiatry* 135:539–42.

Blacker, Carmen. 1975. *The Catalpa Bow: A Study of Shamanistic Practices in Japan*. London: George Allen and Unwin.

Bourguignon, Erika, ed. 1973. *Religion, Altered States of Consciousness, and Social Change*. Columbus: Ohio State University Press.

———. 1976. *Possession*. San Francisco: Chandler and Sharp.

Brendsma, Jeffrey M., and Ludwig, Arnold M. 1974. A Case of Multiple Personality: Diagnosis and Therapy. *International Journal of Clinical and Experiential Hypnosis* 22:216–33.

Caul, David. 1983. Multiple Personalities. Collection of Manuscripts.

Chagnon, Napoleon A. 1977. *Yąnomamö: The Fierce People*. 2d ed. New York: Holt, Rinehart, and Winston.

Colson, Elizabeth. 1969. Spirit Possession among the Tonga of Zambia. In *Spirit Mediumship and Society in Africa*, ed. John Beattie and John Middleton. New York: Africana.

Cross, Whitney R. 1950. *The Burned-Over District: The Social and Intellectual History of Enthusiastic Religion in Western New York*. Ithaca, N.Y.: Cornell University Press.

Davis, Winston. 1980. *Dojo: Magic and Exorcism in Modern Japan*. Stanford, Calif.: Stanford University Press.

Diószegi, Vilmos. 1958. *A Sámánhit Emlékei a Magyar Népi Műveltségben*. Budapest: Akadémiai Kiadó.

Döring, Alois. 1985. Dämonen geben Zeugnis: Teufelsglaube und Exorzismus in traditionalistischen Bewegungen. *Schweizer Archiv für Volkskunde* 81:1–23.

Doyle, Arthur C. 1926. *The History of Spiritualism*. New York: George H. Doran.

Eliade, Mircea. 1964. *Shamanism: Archaic Techniques of Ecstasy*. Princeton: Princeton University Press. Originally published in French as *Le*

Chamanisme et les techniques archaiques de l'extase, 1951, Paris: Librairie Pyot, translated by Willard R. Trask.

Fair, Charles M. 1963. *The Physical Foundations of the Psyche*. Middletown, Conn.: Wesleyan University Press.

Fiedler, Leslie A. 1968. *The Return of the Vanishing American*. New York: Stein and Day.

Figge, Horst F. 1973. *Geisterkult, Besessenheit und Magie in der Umbanda-Religion in Brasilien*. Freiburg: Alber.

Finkler, Kaja. 1985. *Spiritualist Healers in Mexico: Successes and Failures of Alternative Therapeutics*. South Hadley, Mass.: Bergin and Garvey.

Gehrts, Heino. 1962. Jakob Dürr aus Türkheim, der letzte deutsche Schamane. In *Der Teckbote*, 16 June.

———. 1963. Der Schneider von Kirchheim. In *Der Teckbote*, 16 November.

Glazier, Stephen D. 1977. Pentecostalism, Exorcism, and Modernization. Paper presented to the Annual Meeting of the American Anthropological Association, Houston, Texas, 6 January.

Goodman, Felicitas D. 1972. *Speaking in Tongues: A Cross-Cultural Study of Glossolalia*. Chicago: University of Chicago Press.

———. 1974. Disturbances in the Apostolic Church: A Trance-Based Upheaval in Yucatán. In *Trance, Healing, and Hallucination: Three Field Studies in Religious Exerience*, by Felicitas D. Goodman, Jeannette H. Henney, and Esther Pressel, New York: Wiley Interscience.

———. 1974. Possible Physiological Mechanisms for Some Cases of Faith Healing. *Medikon* 3(6/7):39–41.

———. 1981. States of Consciousness: A Study of Soundtracks. *Journal of Mind and Behavior* 2:209–219.

———. 1981. *The Exorcism of Anneliese Michel*. New York: Doubleday.

———. 1986. Body Posture and the Religious Altered State of Consciousness: An Experimental Investigation. *Journal of Humanistic Psychology* 26:81–118.

———. Forthcoming. *Ecstasy, Ritual, and Alternate Reality: Religion in a Pluralistic World*. Bloomington: Indiana University Press.

Grad, Bernard. 1965. Some Biological Effects of the "Laying on of Hands." A Review of Experiments with Animals and Plants. *Journal of Parapsychology* 29:95–129.

Haider, Frank W.; Spong, P.; and Lindsley, D. B. 1964. Attention, Vigilance, and Cortical Evoked Potentials in Humans. *Science* 145:180.

Herbert, W. 1982. The Three Brains of Eve: EEG Data. *Science News* 121:356.

Herskovits, Melville J. 1971. *Life in a Haitian Valley*. Garden City, N.Y.: Doubleday.

Judah, J. Stillson. 1967. *The History and Philosophy of the Metaphysical Movements in America*. Philadelphia: Westminster Press.

Kardec, Allen. 1875. *The Spirit's Book*. Boston: Colby and Rich.

1985. *Katechismus Katholischer Erwachsenen: Das Glaubensbekenntnis der Kirche*. Bonn: Deutsche Bischofskonferenz, Verband der Diözesen Deutschlands.

Kenney, M. G. 1981. Multiple Personality and Spirit Possession. *Psychiatry* 44: 337–58.

Kerner, Justinus. N.d. Geschichte Besessener neuerer Zeit. In *Sämtliche Werke*, ed. Walter Heichen, vol. 2, pp. 69–92.

La Barre, Weston. 1970. *The Ghost Dance: The Origins of Religion*. Garden City, N.Y.: Doubleday.

Lancaster, E. 1958. *The Final Face of Eve*. New York: McGraw-Hill.

Lawton, George. 1932. *The Drama of Life after Death: A Study of Spiritualist Religion.* New York: Henry Holt.

Lee, Richard B. 1968. The Sociology of !Kung Bushman Trance Performances. In *Trance and Possession States,* ed. Raymond Prince, pp. 35–54. Montreal: R. M. Bucke Memorial Society.

Lex, Barbara W. 1979. The Neurobiology of Ritual Trance. In *The Spectrum of Ritual: A Biogenetic Structural Analysis,* ed. Eugene d'Aquili, pp. 117–51. New York: Columbia University Press.

Ludwig, Arnold M. 1968. Altered States of Consciousness. In *Trance and Possession States,* ed. Raymond Prince, pp. 69–95. Montreal: R. M. Bucke Memorial Society.

McNeil, W. K. 1971. Mrs. F.-Little Joe: The Multiple Personality Experience and the Folklorist. *Indiana Folklore* 4:216–45.

Martin, David, and Mullen, Peter, eds., 1984. *Strange Gifts.* Oxford: Basil Blackwell.

Martin, Malachi. 1976. *Hostage to the Devil: The Possession and Exorcism of Five Living Americans.* New York: Reader's Digest Press.

Métraux, Alfred. 1959. *Voodoo in Haiti.* London: André Deutsch.

Mischo, Johannes, and Niemann, Ulrich. 1983. Die Besessenheit der Anneliese Michel (Klingenberg) in interdisziplinärer sicht. *Zeitschrift für Parapsychologie und Grenzgebiete der Psychologie* 25:129–93.

Moody, Raymond. 1975. *Life after Life.* New York: Bantam Books.

Nichol, John Thomas. 1971. *The Pentecostals.* New York: Harper and Row.

Oesterreich, Traugott K. 1974. *Possession and Exorcism,* trans. D. Ibberson. New York: Causeway.

Pressel, Esther. 1974. Umbanda Trance and Possession in São Paulo, Brazil. In *Trance, Healing, and Hallucination: Three Field Studies in Religious Experience,* by Felicitas D. Goodman, Jeannette H. Henney, and Esther Pressel, pp. 113–226. New York: Wiley Interscience.

Putnam, Frank W. et al. 1983. 100 Cases of Multiple Personality Disorder. Paper presented to the American Psychiatric Association Annual Meeting, New Research Abstract #77, New York, 30 April–6 May.

———. 1984. The Psychophysiologic Investigation of Multiple Personality Disorder: A Review. *Psychiatric Clinics of North America* 7:31–39.

———. 1985. Dissociation as a Response to Extreme Trauma. In *Childhood Antecedents of Multiple Personality,* ed. R. P. Klupf, pp. 66–97. Washington, D.C.: APA Press.

Rice, L. 1938. Disintegrated Personalities?—Or Possession? *Journal of the American Society for Psychical Research* 32:69–80.

Rodewyk, Adolf. 1975. *Possessed by Satan,* trans. Martin Ebon. New York: Doubleday. Originally published in German as *Dämonische Besessenheit,* 1963, Aschaffenburg: Patloch.

———. 1976. *Dämonische Besessenheit heute, Tatsachen und Deutungen.* 4th ed. Stein am Rhein: Christiana.

Rosenbaum, Milton, and Weaver, Glenn M. 1980. Dissociated State: Status of a Case after 38 Years. *Journal of Nervous and Mental Disease* 168:597–603.

Schwarz, P. M. 1976. *Teufel, Dämonen, Besessene: Das Reich der Finsternis.* Wien: Kreuz Verlag.

Sherill, John L. 1964. *They Speak with Other Tongues.* New York: McGraw-Hill.

Smith, M. Justa. 1972. Paranormal Effects on Enzyme Activity. *Human Dimensions* 1(2):15–19.

Storl, Wolf-Dieter. 1974. Shamanism among Americans of European Origin. Dissertation, University of Bern (Switzerland).

———. 1983. Die Indianer der Spiritisten. *Wiener Ethnohistorische Blätter*, no. 26:3–18.

Thigpen, Corbett H., and Cleckley, Hervey M. 1957. *The Three Faces of Eve*. New York: McGraw-Hall.

Thomsen, Harry. 1963. *The New Religions of Japan*. Rutland, Vt.: Charles E. Tuttle.

Varma, V. K.; Bouri, M.; and Wig, N. N. 1981. Multiple Personality in India: Comparison with Hysterical Possession State. *American Journal of Psychotherapy* 35:113–20.

Walsh, Roger. 1980. The Consciousness Disciplines and the Behavioral Sciences: Questions of Comparison and Assessment. *American Journal of Psychiatry* 137:663–73.

White, James W. 1970. *The Sōkagakkai and Mass Society*. Stanford, Calif.: Stanford University Press.

Wicke, J. D.; Donchin, E.; and Lindsey, D. B. 1964. Visual Evoked Potential as a Function of Flash Luminance and Duration. *Science* 146:83.

Williams, Cyril G. 1981. *Tongues of the Spirit*. Cardiff: University of Wales Press.

Worsley, Peter. 1968. *The Trumpet Shall Sound*. New York: Schocken.

Zaretsky, Irving I. 1974. In the Beginning Was the Word: The Relationship of Language to Social Organization in Spiritualist Churches. In *Religious Movements in Contemporary America*, ed. Irving I. Zaretsky and Mark P. Leone, pp. 166–213. Princeton: Princeton University Press.

INDEX